Family
Business

When Business is Family and
Family is Business

Dr. Cheryl LeJewell Jackson

DEDICATION

Family Business is dedicated to my parents, Ray and Kay Sanders who continue to show me what it means to put your heart and soul into both your family *and* your family business. It was through our family business that I caught the entrepreneurial spirit that still defines my life today. I love you!

Family Business

DR. CHERYL LEJEWELL JACKSON

CONTENTS

INTRODUCTION

A few years ago, I was sitting in front of my computer staring at two lines of a book I had been working on all day. To be honest, I had been *working* on it for a decade but never got around to actually *writing* it. I had gone from a cushy corporate career to doing consulting work from home so I could finally pursue my dream of spending the best part of my day with my boys while working flexible jobs around that. My boys had been surprisingly good all day, and my mother-in-law had been watching them since early that morning. I had been sitting at my desk since nine in the morning. It was now eleven-thirty, and I was still staring at the first two lines on a blank page. I had no outside distractions, no deadlines, and an entire day to focus entirely on what I wanted to focus on. Yet, in two hours, I was able to type two whole sentences. They weren't even long sentences. If I'm being honest, I believe one sentence was the title and its tagline.

If this had been work for one of my consulting clients, I'd have had it typed up, formatted beautifully, and submitted for final review by now. I was often reprimanded for turning in work too quickly which "set a bad precedent" and "set the bar too high". One of my graduate professors talked about this phenomenon in factory work wherein someone might get a wrench to the back of the head for "showing up" the rest of the team.

Although it was never my intention to show anyone up, as I advanced in my career, I certainly began to understand having priorities outside of finishing the work as quickly as possible.

In my career, I had been successful. Really successful by outside standards. I helped Fortune 50 companies hire and develop top talent to ensure their organizations flourished for another generation. I *did* things. I was *important*. I made a *difference*. Yet, here I sat in front of my computer for two whole hours unable to type more than one complete sentence. Instead, I scrolled through Facebook until I was reading stories I read three weeks ago. I accidentally bumped the screen and sent my feed whirling back to the top, at which point I set it down and looked back at the screen. I checked my Gmail, my other Gmail, my work account, my "info" account, my other Gmail account (yes…that's three). I checked the same accounts on my phone, just in case something was different, and then I checked them once again on the computer. I moved everything from my Google calendar to my paper calendar and then filled the pages of my goal planner just in case I was tempted to be productive over a hair appointment for my son. I sanitized my keyboard and checked in on my mom. I checked the mail, cleared off a corner of my desk, changed out the sheets on my bed, got a snack, and put the bottle of wine back in the fridge after rolling it around in my hands for three minutes while I debated on whether or not this was considered a "vacation" day, in which case drinking by ten in the morning is within reason.

During my years in the corporate world, commuting to and from a freezing office building, I would fantasize about working from home. Oh, how productive I would be! With no one telling me when to work, where to work, how to work, and what to work on, I would be able to fulfill my life's purpose and live my passion. I would have the discipline and focus to work between naps all while spending quality time with my boys. Yet, here I sat with a title and an opening sentence. I began to wonder how I was ever successful. Was I *actually* ever successful? Did I ever really *do* anything with my life? Am I even remembering anything correctly? If I was so successful working for someone else, why was it so hard to be successful at home? Why couldn't I apply that same discipline to my passion and my business?

As I sat there staring at that (almost) blank page, it finally hit me. I had spent fifteen years creating and implementing practices that helped organizations run more effectively, but when it came to my personal business, I thought I could just "wing it". I thought if I was passionate enough, I would just *want* to do it. Perhaps if the desire was strong enough, it would come naturally. If I was *meant* to do it, then it wouldn't be this hard. In reality, that simply is not the case. I was actually living the dream I had always imagined for myself. Granted, I envisioned it at the successful point, but I was on my way. I was literally living a picture-perfect version of my dream. Yet somehow, it didn't *feel* like my dream. I was frustrated that I wasn't excited. I was agitated all the time, mostly at myself, but that didn't stop me from taking it out on everyone else. And I was just really down. I started to question everything about myself: my abilities, my successes, and even my own dreams. I had so many expectations for what life would be like once I got there. Without someone telling me what to do, without the tools and processes to snap me back, I allowed my disappointments to derail me from success.

Whether you have built a growing business with teams of employees or you're just getting started with a dream for a blog, there are tried and true business practices that, I believe, can transform the way you see the work that you do. Collectively, organizations spend billions of dollars every year in developing, implementing, and maintaining practices and programs that allow them to run efficiently, monitor progress, and accomplish goals in alignment with their strategic business initiatives. They are not secrets reserved for the biggest corporations but practices that you can implement in your own small business, your growing dream, or within your own family. When you treat your life like a business, you are able to increase productivity, reduce stress, and function more effectively. A side effect I have found too is the ability to remove the emotion that I allowed to control me as soon as I woke up in the morning. Perhaps all of these practices won't apply to your situation, and that's okay. Take what you like, and leave the rest.

This book is organized by some of the myths I have heard women, just like you and me, say about their businesses. I have said many, if not all of these myself and know how damaging they can be to achieving your goals. Instead of patting ourselves, and each other, on the back, we tear ourselves down. Maybe it isn't what you expected, but that doesn't mean it's bad. My goal is simply to help you be the best you can be and maintain a little sanity along the way.

I was talking to a friend of mine once about how I sometimes felt like a failure as a parent. I often speak in extremes because I believe most people share similar feelings from time to time, and I want them to know they aren't alone. When I paused for a breath she asked, "How often do you feel like a failure as a mom?" I thought for a moment and said, "About three times a day." After seeing her reaction I asked, "Do you ever feel like a failure?" It didn't take much thought before she responded, "Not really, no." So, you may relate to all of these myths, a few, or absolutely none. If you have never had these doubts or fears run through your mind, please do not feel like I am suggesting that you should or that they should be *this* extreme. I was so happy that my friend had never experienced those feelings of failure, and I would delight in knowing that I am the only one who has ever felt this way about my business or family at one point or another. Unfortunately, I know I am not alone in some of these thoughts. My goal is simply to highlight a few of these myths and replace them with the truth. The first truth being, "You are awesome! You got this Momma. You're doing it, and you're doing great!"

MOTIVATION

Myth 1: If I'm living my dream, I should just *want* to do it all the time.

Truth 1: What inspires you to start something will not always push you to take the next step.

We have romanticized the notion of "following your dream". It does not mean you will wake up every morning like you just stepped out of a mattress commercial. Sometimes you would prefer to watch television, swim at the beach, or sleep in. In fact, all of these activities are likely part of your dream. In reality, it takes an extreme amount of discipline to succeed at your dreams.

Man, this was big for me. I was so sure of my purpose when I was working that corporate j-o-b. As a side note, I use the term "j-o-b" throughout this book to describe the work we do for someone else. This work is simply paying the bills but doesn't hold a lot of meaning or fulfillment for us. It doesn't light your fire, but it is still an integral part of the greater plan and the path that was divinely created for you. I don't mean to devalue this work. In fact, this work can be in perfect alignment with God's purpose for your life, which is bringing Christ to your generation. He may have placed you in that *very* spot to reach someone there. I absolutely believe that and encourage women to serve that greater purpose where they are. This book, though, is about your big dreams and businesses. Absolutely grow and serve God where you are. While you are there, you can still pursue your desires that lie just beyond where you are. I am simply trying to differentiate the work that constitutes your dream or small business and the work that may be serving as a stepping stone.

As I was working my corporate j-o-b, I felt in my heart that I wouldn't be there forever. One day I would pursue my passion, and I just *knew* that I would be so motivated if I just had the opportunity to chase it. Sure I could have started doing something back then, but in my mind, if only I had 24 hours a day to work *my* business, motivation would not be an issue. I'm sure you've heard the phrase, "When you're doing what you love, you'll never have to work another day in your life." I just knew one day I would have that feeling; I just needed to find it.

Talk about setting unrealistic expectations! I love my kids. I really do, but somedays, I just don't want to do it. You know those days where you fight with them all morning and finally get them locked, I mean safely secured in their car seats? On those days, I wonder if I'm ever going to get from the rear passenger door to the driver's door. I walk like I'm avoiding going to the principal's office. The last thing I want to do is open that door and hear them screaming at me. I just don't want to do it.

I get so frustrated and begin to doubt myself. Does that mean I made the wrong decision? No way! Does that mean I would change it if given the chance? Heck no! It just means sometimes, I don't want to do it. Not every email is enjoyable. Not every diaper smells like roses. There are always parts of the job, the business, parenting, that you don't want to do, or you just don't feel up to doing it today. That's when discipline kicks in. As parents, we just keep going because we don't really have an option. The kids have to eat. The diaper has to be changed. If you don't get up and drive them to school, then you won't be able to drop them off (and have the day to yourself). Sometimes you just have to push through those tough moments because they come with it.

When I started graduate school, I was beyond excited. I was embarking on the final leg of the race to earn my doctorate degree. Although the road ahead was long, I had an excitement that carried me through five years of classes, papers, exams, my thesis, an internship, and the first 90% of my dissertation. Not every day was easy and not every class held my attention. I certainly didn't sing through my papers and often needed a little help from my little red friend, Shiraz, to get through some meetings with my advisor. Overall, though, knowing the outcome and striving for that goal kept me going most days. The dissertation phase is when the coursework is completed, the comprehensive exam has been passed, and only the inspired research study, 100-page paper, and public defense of your study remains. All of this is often done after leaving the campus and entering the workforce

Although my excitement for this last step in the process started strong, toward the end, I couldn't even bring myself to say the word "dissertation". To read my own writing was painful and often made me physically ill. With each round of edits, it took everything I had to not just accept any changes my advisor suggested. I could see the finish line ahead, but I had hit a wall. At one point I actually thought, "This is good enough. I came close enough; I don't really need to finish it." Regardless of how much you love something, sometimes you just don't want to do it.

The Oxford Learner's Dictionaries defines self-discipline as "the ability to make yourself do something, especially something difficult or unpleasant".[1] The definition itself suggests that it isn't always easy. My son was going down a big twisty slide. He looked at me and said, "Mommy, I'm scared." I said, "It's okay to be scared. You can't be brave if you aren't scared first." Just like bravery, you can't be disciplined without first the temptation to be distracted. John Wooden, NBA player and head coach at the University of California said, "Discipline yourself and others won't need to." I find it motivating to twist it slightly and say, "Discipline yourself or someone else will." This often keeps me working when I would rather sit on the couch. It keeps me pushing when I would rather go to bed. For me, not going back into the workforce is a motivating factor contributing to my self-discipline. Although it is a strong factor, it certainly isn't the only motivating factor.

When it comes to motivation, some people believe that motivation is external. The thought is that motivation merely gets you amped up, but it quickly burns out. It takes something much deeper to keep pushing after the fanfare and excitement has worn out. This is absolutely true. I talk throughout this book about the importance of meaning and your deeper reasons for doing what you do. This drive to push long past the initial excitement or external reward is also a form of motivation. According to psychologists, there are two different types of motivation.

The first type of motivation is extrinsic motivation. This is when motivation comes from external sources or rewards. For many people working for someone else, this comes in the form of a paycheck, promotion, or recognition. Often employees are motivated not by the work itself but by what completion of the work will earn them. When one is extrinsically motivated, the removal of those external rewards stops the motivation to perform the task. If you have heard the phrase, "When the cat's away the mice will play," that is suggesting that when the giver of the motivation is gone, the motivation to do the work is also gone. If you are driven by extrinsic motivation, it will be very difficult for your business or passion to take off. Without income that provides enough motivation and without someone observing your work, you may struggle to keep doing it.

If you feel this may be the case for you, I would recommend you re-evaluate if you are on the right path. Working based on extrinsic motivation is not sustainable. As I mentioned before, some tasks are not enjoyable without the reward of getting to do the rest. Don't let this confuse you into thinking you are on the wrong path. To know your motivation, look at the bigger picture. Where does your motivation sit for the work as a whole? Don't look at the individual tasks or you may not see the big picture.

The second and strongest form of motivation is intrinsic motivation. This is the motivation that comes from the joy or pleasure from doing the task itself. I see raising kids as falling in this category since the motivation comes from the joy of seeing those sweet smiles and feeling so connected to such tiny people. When you are writing content, creating products, or offering a service that you truly enjoy or feel passionately about, regardless of whether or not you receive any appreciation, you are operating under intrinsic motivation. This doesn't mean you don't enjoy appreciation; it's just that your primary driver is the work itself. The saying I mentioned earlier is focused on this intrinsic motivation. "When you do what you love, you will never work another day in your life." This is suggesting that the work itself is intrinsically motivating to you. You are not working for the reward or external praise but for the joy of the work itself. In that sense, the work is no longer....work.

Intrinsic motivation is a critical component of flow, a Positive

Psychology concept developed by Mihály Csíkszentmihályi (pronounced Chick-sent-me-high) in 1975. The theory states that flow is the state of being so involved in your work that time stands still. You are so engaged in your work that you don't notice the distractions around you. Your mind, body, and spirit are fully focused on the task you are doing. You don't notice hunger, thirst, or boredom. I will get into this later when I talk about Positive Psychology, but I wanted to help tie the concepts together here. Although this is a goal for the work that you do, not every part of the work will put you in a state of flow. There are parts of the work that aren't as enjoyable or engaging as others. Somethings just must be done. Although the ultimate goal will be to reduce these tasks as much as possible so you can focus on those that are the most intrinsically motivating, do not be discouraged by the lack of desire for these tasks. Stay focused on the bigger picture and keep your "why" front and center.

I want to touch briefly on an overwhelming and constant lack of motivation. If you find yourself *never* wanting to do the work or *constantly* feeling overwhelmed by your children, you may be dealing with something bigger than a lack of motivation. Depression has many symptoms, one big one being a lack of motivation. You just don't feel like doing *anything*. Many people assume it is natural to dislike work and will keep going. People tend to think raising kids is exhausting, and they keep pushing through despite an overwhelming sense of exhaustion and/or dread. When things get too difficult or the symptoms become obvious to others, they finally seek help.

I encourage you to pay attention and seek help if you feel that your lack of motivation may indeed be a symptom of depression. You may not have severe depression, but it can quickly spiral. Think of depression as a spectrum with varying degrees. You don't have to be at the far end to benefit from getting help. Even your j-o-b shouldn't be a daily struggle to get out of bed. Sometimes leaving a bad j-o-b or relationship will fix the problem, but sometimes that's not the case. Depression is bigger than changing your situation, though if you are in a bad j-o-b or relationship, I absolutely encourage you to find a way out. Take a look inside and evaluate your unique situation. If you suffer from a lingering lack of motivation, please take care of yourself and ask a medical professional for help.

In the Time Management section, we will talk about these things you don't want to do and how to actually, well, not do them. In this section, I just wanted you to understand some of the psychology behind those tasks you don't love and know that it is absolutely okay and expected to not love every bit of your business or even your dream as a whole.

Summary:

- The excitement that got you started on your dream may not always be there to get you through the hard times.

- Intrinsic motivation is the key to living your dream.

- Depression can also look like a lack of motivation. Seek professional help if you experience intense and consistent lack of motivation.

CHALLENGES

Myth 2: If I'm living my dream or purpose, it shouldn't be *this* hard.

Truth 2: Just about anything worth doing is going to be hard from time to time…and maybe even most of the time. Wow. Talk about a downer.

"I knew it would be hard, I just didn't think it would be *this* hard." I was talking to my friend one day, and I said this about having children. It hit me that I had the same thought about following my business dreams. As much as I love my boys, raising them is *hard*. Most of the time it is way harder than I thought it would or *should* be. Sometimes we have the thought that if we are following our passion, it should come naturally; it should be easy. Although it is often the case that you are passionate about something that you also happen to be really good at, that is not always the case. I have learned that I am passionate about many things. I tend to hear a cool research study and want to change my entire focus. Passion can be very fluid, and it doesn't always clearly align with your strengths.

There are also parts of the dream where you have exceptional gifts and others that pose a greater challenge. I am a gifted nurturer, but disciplining my children is another story. That doesn't mean I should throw in the towel on this whole mommy thing. It also doesn't mean I shouldn't try to improve in that area. You can certainly grow your proficiency in a given area. People do this all the time. In fact, that learning process can be very inspired, resulting in a successful state of flow (the state of intense focus and enjoyment I mentioned earlier). It can also be a bit of a struggle as the proficiency develops. It is usually harder to move the needle on a weakness than a strength or even something that falls in between. It can be enjoyable to make small tweaks and see significant improvement. Weaknesses are more challenging. It takes more focus and prolonged energy to see improvement, which can be very discouraging. Therefore, don't focus only on these weaknesses. Spend some energy developing in other areas as well. This will be more encouraging for you.

There is also a side of running your own business or side-hustle that you don't always account for. That is the disappointment and the struggle of making progress. It doesn't always come easily. There aren't always people lined up to buy your product/service or read your blog. It can be discouraging and disappointing. It can make you wonder if you made the right decision. Sometimes you work harder than you have ever worked before. You watch your family doing things without you. That's hard. Sometimes your spouse doesn't share your passion and may question why you are spending so much time working on your business. It can cause arguments and really test your relationships. These are the times I wonder if it's harder than it should be or if I am somehow *making* it harder than it should be. Sometimes, it's just hard. That does not mean you're on the wrong track.

When you change your mindset to accepting that this is indeed part of the process, it is easier to "go with the flow" and not get caught up in trying to change it or wish it away. Sure, I wish my kids didn't pick on each other or throw temper tantrums in the middle of the grocery store. We are indeed working on it, but by recognizing that this is merely part of the process of learning and growing, then it's easier to not get so hung up on it. Rather than getting twisted over it, I can lean into my knowledge of how to handle the situation and take it one step at a time. Finding joy even in the hard times allows you to more fully enjoy the good times. When you decided to pursue a dream, you may have only thought about the good times, but it's all one big package. Don't worry so much about being on the wrong track and know that this is all just part of it. It's just like a marriage. We say, "for better or worse" for a reason, and that's because there will indeed be better and worse seasons. It's all just part of it, but that's what makes it all so beautiful.

I also want to touch on the idea that being hard is a bad thing. Our brains are wired to think that things that are difficult are bad. The part of our brain aimed at keeping us alive is the fastest processing one, processing data at a speed of 20 million bits per second.[2] When it sees danger, it diverts us. When it feels pain, it runs. When something gets hard, it slams on the brakes. The conscious part of our brain aimed at self-actualization and growth is much slower. It processes information at 40 bits per second.[2] That means that the part of the brain screaming "Avoid!" is operating 500,000 times faster than the part of the brain that thinks exploring something new would be fun. The conscious part of the brain is only responsible for processing about .01% of the data that comes through our brains.[2] That is a *lot* of data being filtered out by our subconscious, over-protective brain. By the time our conscious mind is giving the "all clear", the protective side has hit the ejector button. It actually sends signals to our bodies resulting in physiological change. Increased heart rate, sweating, and dry mouth are physiological responses to fear, danger, and excitement. We have been conditioned to evaluate these responses as fear. Therefore, our response is to try to avoid it.

When something gets hard, we often respond with fear. We don't give ourselves time to sit with that feeling and reprogram our brains to encode the "hard" as "exciting" or even "okay". When I used to try out for the all-region band in high school, I was usually pretty nervous. I would get quiet, pace back and forth, and get super jittery. I didn't want to talk to anyone. My mom would always say, "Nerves are a good thing,". and they are. They help you stay alert and improve your reaction time. By channeling our nerves into excitement, we gain the benefits of being nervous without the reaction of "flight" (a.k.a., run).

Prior to one of these events, my private lesson teacher told me to take slow, deep breaths when I got nervous. This practice is two-fold. Slowing down and focusing on your breathing takes your attention off of the anxiety-inducing activity in front of you. Thoughts in your brain can be like a tornado. It starts innocent enough, but before you know it, it has spiraled out of control. Stopping to breathe serves to interrupt the spiraling, replacing it with something calming.

Secondly, deep breathing exercises increase oxygen to the brain. This has been shown to reduce stress hormones in the body while increasing dopamine levels in the brain. Dopamine is responsible for activating the reward centers in the brain. This is why it is often used in anti-depressant medications. Substances causing an increase in dopamine have also been linked to addiction for these same reasons and should be used with caution. Dopamine also plays an important role in movement, sleep, learning, mood, memory, attention, and is a natural pain reliever. Through the release of oxygen and increases in dopamine, deep breathing helps increase feelings of calm and well-being. Once you have triggered this reaction, you are better equipped to approach the situation from a place of peace. At this point, you can reframe your feelings from fear to excitement or counteract the physiological responses all together, resulting in a more calm response.

One summer, my family went to an indoor water park. My oldest son was two and a half years old at the time. We were walking into the wave pool when the wave suddenly started up. I expected to ease into the waves, but they came much harder and faster than I thought. Before I could make a plan, we were both underwater. My son was wearing a life jacket, but the waves crashed right over him. We had made it to an odd depth where we were hitting the bottom and I couldn't quite get my feet under me to push us out of the water. We were tumbling for what felt like an eternity. I expected at any moment to feel the soft, delicate hand of the teenage lifeguard pulling us to safety. It didn't happen.

I was finally able to get my feet underneath me and pull us both up and out of the water. Gasping and shaking, I stumbled toward the edge of the pool while the waves crashed around my legs. I looked at my son who was still clearing water away from his eyes. I just knew he was going to be scared and want to leave. Before I could say anything, he grabbed onto my arms and said between breaths, "Big. Waves. Are. *Awesome!*"

I couldn't help but smile at his excitement. That *is* why we went in, right? Floating in the still water is fun for a while, but what makes us go back time and time again are the waves. And isn't life just like that? Some days we are strolling along and the next day we are completely underwater. Isn't it the waves that we remember? It's the struggles that we talk about, and it's in the challenges that we are growing. Without the waves, we wouldn't be ready to take on our next assignment. It's also in the waves that our children are learning to handle their own challenges. It's in these moments that we are actually becoming more like the image of Christ.

I encourage you to stop seeing the hard things as the enemy but see them as preparation for a promotion. This is when we learn what we are really made of. Without the challenge of the hard things, we may never know what we are fully capable of. The hard things give us the confidence to know what we're made of. It isn't always fun, and it is by definition not easy, but man it is so worth it!

Summary:

- The subconscious part of the brain processes information 100 times faster than the conscious part of your brain. Your fear reaction is often just a result of the subconscious brain getting there first. Refocus and reprogram your brain to experience things differently.

- Deep breathing increases dopamine and reduces the stress hormone in your body.

- Recognize that the hard stuff is just part of the dream. It's in the hard stuff that we grow.

SATISFACTION

Myth 3: If I get rid of all of these things that made me dissatisfied at my

j-o-b, I will be satisfied.

Truth 3: Eliminating the things you didn't like about your j-o-b does not necessarily mean you will suddenly feel more satisfied. What is satisfaction anyway?

I just want to start off by saying that most of the field's research on engagement and satisfaction is for employees. As in, how satisfied are you with your j-o-b, this organization, and your team and how engaged are you in your work? There isn't as much money in improving family or business engagement. Unfortunately, that means we don't know a lot about it. That said, I believe there are plenty of insights we can glean from understanding the role of satisfaction and engagement in our workforce.

For a long time, researchers believed "dissatisfaction" and "satisfaction" to be on the same continuum. As in, if you get rid of all of those things causing dissatisfaction in your job (life, marriage, etc.), you will increase your satisfaction. In 1959, Frederick Herzberg sought to better understand job satisfaction. He asked a group of people about their good experiences at work and asked another about their bad. What he found was that people described their good and bad experiences differently. The opposite of the bad experiences did not necessarily equate to good experiences. This ultimately led to the development of his Two-Factor Theory, also referred to as Motivator-Hygiene Theory. The premise is that dissatisfaction and satisfaction are not merely opposite ends of the same scale but in fact *two separate* scales or continuums altogether. He referred to the factors affecting dissatisfaction as "hygiene" factors and those influencing satisfaction, "motivators" or "satisfiers".

According to Herzberg, hygiene factors reduce dissatisfaction, but the best-case scenario is zero dissatisfaction. By improving these factors, one does not necessarily increase in satisfaction. Some hygiene factors are pay, security, policies, work conditions, supervision, and some foundational relationships. These are often referred to as the "contractual" components of your job. Although these components are important and often result in a bump in satisfaction, Herzberg argues that the bump is temporary and will normalize as these factors become an accepted (and expected) part of the job. Many organizations attempt to increase satisfaction and engagement by increasing employee pay, for example. Employees often do feel "happier" and satisfaction may increase, but this increase is artificial and temporary. Soon the additional pay will become a normal operating procedure, and the benefits to satisfaction will be lost. I think of hygiene factors as gas in your car. Filling the tank will result in the car moving forward, but that's about it. If you want enhanced performance or efficiency, you have to do more than simply adding the basics.

I was talking to a girlfriend of mine many years ago. She was struggling in her marriage and opened up about how she just didn't love her marriage.

I knew her husband too, and I knew that he was a pretty great guy. He helped around the house, had a great job, and was great with their son. At that time in my life, I was in a relationship where I had *no* help. In my mind, her spouse was an absolute *dream*! I just could not understand what the issue was. Although having a partner who contributes to the household and fulfills their obligations as a husband, father, and human being living in the home is a great perk and can have a significant impact on overall satisfaction, these components are simply hygiene factors. They are the cost of entry. They are often a requirement to begin the process of satisfaction, but they are not the factors that get you there. These factors merely increase or decrease *dis*satisfaction. I was significantly more dissatisfied in my relationship and ultimately left. She, on the other hand, at least had a foundation to work with. They were eventually able to build upon that foundation and improve the factors that really moved the needle in their relationship. These factors are the motivators.

Motivators or satisfiers are those factors related to satisfaction. These include things like achievement, recognition, the work itself, responsibility, advancement, growth, and advanced relationships. Despite a negative account on the hygiene side, employees may find themselves satisfied and motivated at work because of a sufficient amount of these factors. You may experience this in your small business when the money is not there, security is not there, your relationships are suffering, and so on. Your hygiene factors may be low, but you are highly satisfied because of the motivator factors. You enjoy the work you are doing and you have a sense of achievement, responsibility, and growth.

In the example I mentioned earlier with my friend and her marriage, she was not getting the factors that contributed to her overall satisfaction. As often happens when couples have children, their relationship took a bit of a dip. Raising a child requires a great deal of physical, mental, and emotional energy. When you give your energy to one thing, you take it away from something else. This is often the relationship between the husband and wife. With less time and energy to spend on one another, there is less opportunity to give each other what is needed most. For my friend, this was emotional intimacy that comes with spending time together outside of the hustle and bustle of morning and evening routines. Even if her spouse wasn't great at doing the dishes or taking out the trash without being prompted, a full tank of emotional intimacy would have carried her through for quite some time. When addressing the hygiene factors, she would have been able to do so from a more emotionally stable position. Motivators contribute to a sense of purpose and belonging that drives one's feeling of satisfaction.

Many researchers and practitioners use the terms "satisfaction" and "engagement" interchangeably. We talk about satisfaction when what we really want is engagement. Although satisfaction is often difficult to attain, engagement is even more elusive. Herzberg's motivators may indeed lead to increased satisfaction, but that only gets you so far. When I think of the term "satisfied", I think about the 100 diet plans I have tried in my life. Inevitably, the goal is to not eat past the point of being satisfied. Several have even used a diagram of a balloon. You don't want to be a limp, flaccid balloon. That means you're still hungry. You also don't want to be a bulging balloon, because that means you are too full. You want to be a partially filled balloon where you are neither full nor hungry.

I don't know about you, but sometimes, I just want to feel full! And I certainly didn't leave the security of my job and work late into the night just to feel satisfied. I want to feel *full*! I want to be overflowing with excitement. Perhaps those are unrealistic expectations leading to this myth, but I do believe in my heart of hearts that we actually want more than being content, satisfied, neither full nor hungry. I believe we all want to feel fulfilled, passionate, and overflowing. We want to be involved and deeply invested in our work. What we all want to be is engaged. Nowhere is engagement more visible than on the mission field where people give selflessly of themselves because they have such a strong sense of purpose. They are driven by something more powerful than basic needs, achievement, and even the work itself. They are driven by a passion and love for their fellow human beings. When you connect with a greater purpose or meaning, your engagement will push you to do things you never thought possible. Where a *dissatisfied* employee will struggle to do the bare minimum, a *satisfied* employee will be motivated to do a good job, but an *engaged* employee will go above and beyond. When other factors fall short, engagement will carry them through.

It's not always easy to detect when we are settling for satisfied. Comfortable is the killer of great. When things are pretty good, we tend to not push for better. It's easier to sit back and swing in the hammock of calm seas. Although 70% of people in America and 85% of people worldwide hate their jobs, a surprisingly few willingly leave in search of something better.[3] I started my career right before the recession in the early 2000s. As the resident Industrial Psychologist, for years it was my responsibility to support the process of downsizing. Organizations often call it different things: downsizing, rightsizing, layoffs, letting people go, restructuring, etc. Whatever they call it, the result is often hundreds of people losing their jobs in a matter of half a day. I designed the process, followed all the rules, and tried to make it as fair as possible (by legal standards and what employees would perceive as fair). I walked leadership through the process of rating and evaluating each and every employee, and often leadership that didn't even realize that their names were on that list as well. I helped Human Resources teams develop the scripts, taught the managers what to say, and even sat in while they gave the news to the tearful employees. I collected badges at the door and was often the last person the employee saw inside the building. It was rarely easy, though some employees handled the news better than others. As employees handed over their badges and clung to their box of pictures, all hope seemed lost. How could a company they devoted so much time to just let them go like they were a piece of dirt stuck to the bottom of their shoe? It's hard to imagine having so little value. I remember so clearly one employee who had been up until three in the morning finishing a project only to be let go five and a half hours later. Watching so many spirits crushed almost broke me. Although it was always the most devastating part of my j-o-b, I knew something incredible was going to come out of this.

Time after time, I would bump into or hear from someone who was let go during one of these processes. They would tell me how they started a new career or went back to school. One lady told me how she finally had time to start the nonprofit she had only dreamed about for years. Once they were forced out of their j-o-bs, it wasn't so scary to start something new. They didn't have as much to lose, and suddenly, being a little uncomfortable didn't seem so hard. Once they saw how painful the comfort zone really was, they never wanted to go back. Despite the intimate knowledge I had about this, I was reluctant to take that leap. As *un*comfortable as the comfort zone really is, it's so easy to sit there and just wait for something better to come along. I waited until, one day, it was finally my turn. The chopper became the chopped. I was relieved, devastated, terrified, and excited all at the same time. Sometimes, I think God will let us sit there, waiting for us to take the leap. He won't let us sit there forever though. There will come a time when He says, "Enough is enough." He'll take that scratchy old nest you're snuggled up in and flip it right over. When he does, you had better be ready to fly!

Where hygiene factors are contractual, engagement factors are transformational. Transformational means the individual is actually changed as a result of the event, feeling, or factor. Transformational events address all parts of the individual's needs including the heart, spirit, mind, and hands. Engagement factors include meaning, autonomy, growth, impact, and connection. These factors go above and beyond the basic needs of individuals and tap into their deeper purpose. Employees will move mountains when they are engaged. When an employee is disengaged, it will be tough to get them to move a mustard seed if it isn't in their job description. Engagement is a tough concept to fully capture, and satisfaction is a great way to start the discussion and begin to understand what true transformational beliefs would look like. Although engagement is about more than either Hygiene or Motivator factors, these factors form the foundation for engagement. Without a solid base of satisfaction, engagement has a tough time even taking root, much less flourishing.

This discussion of engagement is also in alignment with Maslow's hierarchy of needs which states that our needs follow a certain hierarchy beginning with our basic, physiological need for food, water, breathing, shelter, clothing, and sleep. In the next level are the needs related to Safety and Security: health, employment, property, family, and social stability. Love and Belonging are next with the needs of friendship, family, intimacy, and a sense of connection. It is no coincidence that family is listed twice, first as it pertains to their safety and second as it pertains to the love we receive. Even above love, we are driven to protect them and keep them safe. And that may indeed be the greatest form of love. The next level represents the needs related to Self-Esteem. These include confidence, achievement, respect for others, and the need to be a unique individual. The ultimate goal is to achieve self-actualization, which is at the tip of the triangle. This includes the needs of morality, creativity, spontaneity, acceptance, and the need to experience purpose, meaning, and inner potential. The theory states that we are unable to move up the hierarchy of needs until the needs at the preceding level are met. If you have ever taken a psychology class in high school or college, this is one of the very first psychological theories you learned about. This is because it is so fundamental to our field. It seems so elementary, but it serves as an explanation for so many human behaviors. I find myself regularly referencing this simple triangle of human needs. When it comes to our families and family business, we can't expect our loved ones to jump past their basic needs right away. As supportive as my incredible husband is, if we were unable to pay the bills for extended periods of time or if he couldn't purchase some of his little luxuries (does anyone else have an *avid* reader in the family?) for a while, his engagement with my mission would certainly come into question.

When you take the plunge and start your small business or pursue your passion, it should do more than meet your basic needs and give you a sense of "contentedness". It takes way less energy to go work for someone else. You may have to sell your soul, and it may slowly crush your spirit, but initially, it requires way less energy. If you aren't fired up about what you are doing, then you aren't getting one of the most powerful benefits of working for yourself. I don't mean that you bound out of bed at five am every morning just so excited to get to work. Who are those people anyway?! It may not be easy or enjoyable all of the time, but you should definitely be engaged. You should feel connected to the greater purpose and enjoy the work you are doing. I will talk about this more a bit later, but I wanted to start the conversation here.

I ask you to pause for a moment and take some time to identify your Motivator and Hygiene factors. What are those things that result in dissatisfaction if you don't have them? What are the basic needs you have? Define your Motivators. Really outline what it is that you are getting out of your business or what you want to get out of your business. What would it take for you to be fully engaged with what you are doing? This is often described as your "why". Your why is a very powerful tool for you to use when things get tough. Your Motivators will keep you going long after your Hygiene tank is empty. Really dig into each of the components: Meaning, Autonomy, Growth, Impact, and Connection.

Meaning: What is your greater purpose? Who are you serving and why?

Autonomy: are you enjoying the autonomy of working for yourself? Ability to make your own schedule, decide what projects to take on, and decide who you will work with.

Growth: Is the work challenging for you? Are you growing spiritually, mentally, emotionally, or physically?

Impact: What impact are you having on others or other things?

Connection: Are you connecting with others in meaningful ways? Are you sharing ideas and loving on one another?

Fully tapping into all of these areas will help you tap into your engagement motivation and help answer the question, "Why do I do what I do?" I encourage you to not attempt to answer these questions when you are in the heat of a struggle. I have a friend who runs a bi-annual children's clothing consignment event. If I were to ask her these questions a month before the event and even throughout the event itself, she would probably snap at me and tell me she hated her life. I actually know this to be exactly what she would do. But after the event, when things are calmer and she is writing the checks for the consignors, she would tell me that she is serving the community and helping these moms clear out their homes. Not only do they feel better in a less cluttered home, but they are able to purchase the next season's clothing with the money they made. Some are even able to pay a bill or contribute to their household expenses. Additionally, shoppers in the community are able to purchase high-quality items at a fraction of the cost anywhere else, including driving across town to pick up something at someone's home (which is incredibly dangerous). She truly is serving her community, which is what drives her to keep going. Although she may not always be able to physically vocalize it due to the amount of stress she feels, it is what keeps her doing it year after year.

When things are calm, take the time to go through this list of questions and identify what is really driving you to do what you do. Once you have your list, identify any gaps or areas you can improve to make a difference in your overall satisfaction and engagement.

Summary:

- Satisfaction and dissatisfaction are not on the same scale.

- Engagement, our ultimate goal, is a transformational process tapping into your body, spirit, and mind.

- Self-actualization requires achievement of all needs before it. If you are struggling to feel engagement, evaluate where you stand with each of the previous needs.

ENGAGEMENT

Myth 4: I know how my family feels; I don't need to ask them.

Truth 4: You don't know unless you ask. Actually, this should read, "Truth: Do you ever really know?"

We touched on your engagement with your work or business in the previous section. In this section, I want to talk a bit about understanding and assessing your own, your family or your employee engagement. One thing organizations have begun to do fairly well is conduct "Engagement Surveys". I'm having a hard time not rolling my eyes as I write this, but I ask you to hang with me for a minute. I was often on the team developing them, considering vendors, or working with reporting. I also took the survey every year as a dutiful employee, helped facilitate employee deep-dives afterward, and helped develop leadership action plans. I was regularly on the giving, receiving, beginning, and end of the survey process. Even though I was heavily involved in these surveys, I didn't always enjoy taking them. Being open and honest about your feelings toward someone or your organization can often be difficult, especially if you know it could hurt their feelings, impact their bonus, or result in negative emotion toward you. It requires a lot of thought and vulnerability, and a lot of people aren't willing to do that. If you are the only one on your team expressing challenging emotions, then it can put you in an even worse spot. Encouraging employees to open up is a tough job in itself.

Just in case you have never taken such a survey or have blocked them from your memory, engagement or opinion surveys typically ask questions focused on understanding the workforce attitudes. Although they are often referred to as engagement, culture, or opinion surveys, they are really designed to evaluate all aspects of the employees' experience including factors contributing to satisfaction/dissatisfaction and engagement/ disengagement. Questions are typically asked at the team level (i.e., I have the support I need from my direct supervisor, I feel supported by my co-workers), at the department/business or function level (i.e., My leadership demonstrates organizational values), and at the organizational level (i.e., I would recommend this company to a friend, How likely are you to leave the organization within the next six months?). Data is then reported at the lowest leadership level with at least five total respondents. Needless to say, it is a daunting process but ultimately provides valuable information to managers and leaders who often struggled with implementing anything useful before the next round of surveys ensues. I am in no way suggesting that you implement an engagement survey with your family or business; let me be clear on that. I do, however, think there are some valuable ideas you can pull from this organizational practice.

First of all, organizations do not presume to understand what their employees need or their level of engagement based on the amount of work they are doing. Just because they are doing what you ask in no way means they are happy doing it and not actively interviewing with someone else on their lunch break. If you were gone for a week, would those things get done? It's tough to say. Without asking and getting to the heart of things, it is impossible to fully understand what someone else is feeling or what they believe. Unfortunately, even asking directly won't always get you honest answers. Few people are going to tell their bosses they are actively looking to leave the organization.

Secondly, organizations do not assume that just because it was great last year that it will be good this year. Attitudes change, needs change, and people change. It is important to evaluate regularly. Again, I do not recommend you surveying your teenager or husband, but this is where family dinners, date nights, and car-ride conversations come into play.

I was doing some shopping, many moons ago. As I was checking out, I was asked a customer service question on the credit card reader. It was just a single question and asked, "Did your cashier smile?" Although many organizations have a link to a survey on their receipt and entice customers to fill it out with free products or coupons, the reality is that a very small percentage of customers actually fill them out. When they do, they tend to be the extremes: highly satisfied or highly dissatisfied. By asking a single question to each customer, they had a significantly higher response rate (it was faster to answer the question than to find a button to close out) and they get a more representative sample of responses from their customers. By asking a single question to each customer, they can eventually build a fairly accurate view of their overall customer satisfaction by store, region, state, or across all stores for a given point in time (and that is key). Organizations have begun implementing a similar process of surveying a smaller group of employees and doing it more often. This is often referred to as a "pulse" survey because it allows leadership to take the "pulse" of the organization without the cost of assessing the entire workforce. It also allows them to ask questions related to specific changes or programs. By asking fewer questions more often, leadership can have an on-going assessment of how the workforce is doing. When an issue pops up, they can more quickly jump into action rather than waiting an entire year to find out it is even an issue.

Similarly, when you have a captive audience or an opportunity, use that time to ask your family questions that assess their satisfaction but really get to the heart of their engagement. When they receive an award at school or make a good grade on a test, ask them how they felt about earning the reward. What did it mean to them? What was the significance? Ask them about their friends and other relationships. If they are particularly interested in a topic or sport, dig into that; really understand *why* they enjoy it so much. If you have employees, sit down with them one-on-one to talk about their engagement factors (meaning, autonomy, growth, impact, and connection). Are there areas you could adjust to help increase engagement for them? Just knowing you care enough to ask goes a long way, but don't stop there. I will talk about the importance of action in a moment.

Many engagement surveys over the years have revealed a significant lack of meaning for employees. This has resulted in the development of more clearly defined organizational values, and also the implementation of volunteer days. This is where employees either gather together to serve a particular organization as a group or they can volunteer at their organization of choice for a certain number of hours a year. Through this practice, employees build a sense of meaning and connection that often spills over to the organization. As altruistic as many organizations claim, this, along with the impressive public relations benefit, is the primary reason for their great sacrifice. None the less, leaders in organizations are beginning to see the benefit of improved engagement in their workforce and are taking steps to implement real, value-add change. And it's not just good for organizations but also applies to families.

Getting your children and spouse involved in their community is a great way to help foster meaning and purpose into their lives as well. It gives them an opportunity to contribute to something bigger than themselves, giving them a greater sense of purpose all around. This effect is magnified when you do it together. I will talk more about meaning and the powerful effect it can have on your overall wellbeing later in this book. For now, I just want you to understand that meaning and purpose can be very powerful driving forces for your family as well as small businesses.

As you think through exactly how to tap into your family or employees' engagement, I want to highlight some critical components. I cannot over-emphasize the importance of being specific about the area(s) of interest. Some people like to be sneaky and approach the real issue from various angles. In organizations, we have begun to move away from this approach as it just doesn't have the same results as asking directly. You may think you're being sneaky, but either people know exactly what you are asking for and get annoyed at your attempt to trick them or they have no idea what you are getting at and give feedback that is completely irrelevant to what you are asking for. Either way, it is not ideal for truly understanding the environment. In organizations, when we asked about "your leadership", we were very specific as to *which* level of leadership we were talking about. You may be asking your children about "our parenting", but they may struggle with how to respond. In order to trigger feedback in their brains, they need specific hooks to get them started. "When Mommy put you in timeout..." or "When Daddy picks you up from school...", They need to be able to provide clear and specific feedback to each of you.

Next, ask for specific feedback about what you can do to make it better. Actionable is key! You may *think* you know what they need based on their struggle, but maybe you don't. More time with you may mean vacation to you but a quiet dinner to them. This is about *them*, not you and how you always thought it would be. Let go of your expectations and know that the end result will still be amazing if you put in the effort to understand. As you receive feedback, be open to hearing things that hurt or things that go against what you expected to hear. You may be planning elaborate family vacations, but your kids may just want to stay home. Better yet, they may just want some *say* in where you go. Some feedback will be easy to hear while other feedback may be tough.

I want to talk a moment about the critical role of action. What we discovered across large corporations and small teams alike was the simple act of asking went a long way to making employees feel heard, but it wasn't enough. After years of asking and letting results sit on a shelf or tackling only the "easy" issues, employees lost trust in their leadership. Rather than increasing engagement, the surveys themselves began to result in a decrease in engagement. This leads us to the final thing we can learn from this organizational process, and that is to do something with the information you have. The number one most frustrating thing we heard from employees was not the time it took to take the questionnaire, the duplicate questions, or the ridiculous level of detail. They weren't even too concerned about confidentiality or anonymity, which we were always hyper-aware of. The number one thing was whether or not leadership was going to do anything about it. Year after year we heard things like, "They didn't do anything about it last year", "What's the point? None of this matters", "It's not like they actually care". We set up stringent processes of reporting, focus groups, feedback channels, and action planning and barely moved the needle because it was the leadership that needed to show interest; not the project team. It takes an incredible amount of courage to be vulnerable and honest about your feelings toward your team, managers, co-workers, organization, parents, or family. Many people fear retaliation, and rightly so. But even just taking the time to define and speak your feelings is difficult. We found that those who were the least likely to respond were the closest to leaving. They had given up and just didn't care anymore. When someone cares enough to try to make it better, you MUST respect that effort and take action. You may get a second chance, but you aren't likely to get a third. Knowledge truly is power. As much as it may hurt to hear at times, it's the only way to get better. Be sure to use that knowledge to make things better.

Summary:

- Regularly check in with family and team to gauge their engagement.

- Ask specific questions about important areas and even yourself – more specific = more actionable. Get examples of how you can improve or what would help.

- Don't just ask. *Do* something with the information you receive.

EXCITEMENT

Myth 5: Everyone around me will be as excited about my dream as I am.

Truth 5: No one will ever be excited about your dream as you are. Some get close, but it's *your* dream.

One side effect of engagement is that we assume everyone else feels the same way we do. Your dream, purpose, vision is so awesome, how could they not?! This was a major eye-opener for me. As I was writing my first novel, I was typing away by nine in the morning and was still typing at three the next morning. I would spend the morning with my boys, but right after breakfast, I was locked in my room. My husband would bring me lunch and dinner while asking, "Are we ever going to see you again?" I would shake my head and say, "Not today". I knew they would like to see me, and I did miss them, but I was just so excited about what I was doing, I couldn't bring myself to break away. Even when I was with them, I was thinking about my book and counting down the minutes before I could get back to my computer. I certainly didn't consider the impact pursuing my passion had on him or the rest of my family. My husband was carrying a great deal of the load for the extra hours I spent pecking on my computer, all without any of the extra rewards. Sure, he was motivated by seeing me so excited, but that can only carry a guy so long. Your family needs to see the benefit (for *them*) to stay excited. It may sound like a dream-crusher, but unless they are as "transformationally" connected to your work as you are, they aren't getting those incredible benefits that you are receiving. They aren't as intrinsically motivated by the work as you are and need a little more external benefit. Help them see what's in it for them. Make sure to spend special time with them and show your appreciation. They want to be there for you, but you can't expect them to sacrifice freely indefinitely.

Early in my early entrepreneur days, I heard other women talk about the impact their business had on their children. I was single and carefree, so I didn't pay it much mind. Years later, I am beginning to understand how important that really is. It is hard for your family to get too excited about your new venture, especially when it isn't pulling in the money that might "justify" the hours, such as writing your first book. Fortunately, my husband was super supportive. I recognized, though, that when I started working on the second book before the first had taken off, it wasn't as easy to spend hours locked away. The "satisfaction tank" I mentioned earlier was running dry. If the tables were turned (which, unfortunately, they often are with women being on the "extra load" side of the table) what would you need in order to feel okay with the extra time your spouse is spending at work? Is it appreciation? Extra dedicated time each week? The promise of a nice reward when things slow down? Consider asking what your family needs and then commit to doing everything in your power to give it to them.

This is especially true when your business is first getting started or when you are extra excited about the direction. As your family is learning to see less of you or see you differently ("Don't go to work Mommy!"), it is especially important to show your family what's in it for them. When your kids haven't spent as much time with you as they'd like, let them know that you will do something special with them just as soon as this project is over, and make sure that something special is meaningful to them. Many working moms get this confused and think it means "stuff". If we can't spend time with them, we buy them something. I was gone on a long trip; I will bring you back a toy. I worked sixty hours this week; here's that new truck you wanted. What they really want, and need, is your time. Take them to the park, make a special dinner, or take a short vacation. Walk to the sno-cone stand and sit together while you eat it. Whenever you leave or lock yourself in your office, you can remind them of their role in your business. "You were such a good boy! You let Mommy work, and I was able to finish my blog. Now we can go do something fun!" By letting you work, they are making an important contribution to the project. Remind them of the reward you will both get when it is completed.

I was part of a party-based direct sale business many years ago. One of the women on my leadership team said she would give her kids a marble every time she had to leave for a party or make phone calls. When the jar was full, she would take a whole day off and they would spend the entire day together. The number of marbles that filled the jar was based on the number of parties she needed to hold to achieve her next goal. If you are finishing a big project or have given yourself a certain amount of time to complete a deliverable, break the days down into marbles or even a morning and evening marble. "When all of these marbles are gone, we will spend the day at the beach!" That way your kids see their role in your success, and it becomes their success as well. This can not only help them support your new role, but it can teach them valuable lessons about hard work, dedication, and discipline. If you talk to them about your why and your purpose, they start to pick up some of those same values.

In addition to modeling, it is critical to allow children to experience the journey, trials, and victories for themselves. Organizations have begun to capitalize on this method of learning. Instead of simply teaching the principles, research shows that on-the-job learning experience is a great source for learning and more valuable than classroom training.[3] We can teach people material all day, but real learning takes place when they get to experience it for themselves. When your children see you living your values, following your dreams, and pursuing your goals, they begin to emulate those behaviors. That is when true development begins.

I'm not going to go into details on how to keep your spouse "on board". I do, though, want to highlight that it isn't just the special rewards that they need. Your partner needs to know they aren't parenting alone while you pursue your passion and that your dream isn't more important than them. They are, after all, a big part of your dream. You can't just dump all of the responsibilities on them and say, "But I'm doing this for us". This was evident for me in my favorite show *The Office* when Jim left Scranton to pursue his dream leaving his wife Pam working full-time and raising two young children on her own. While he was being driven by limo to play basketball with his idol, she was hauling the trash, sanitizing after lice, and comforting her daughter when Daddy couldn't make the dance recital. Although he was indeed working hard, he had the luxury of following his dream. She, on the other hand, was left keeping the pieces together at home. Despite the fact that they were the "ideal couple" and very much in love, it was tough on their marriage. When he said, "I'm doing this for *us*," I stood up and started yelling at him through the screen. I have seen the show no fewer than 879 times, and it still gets me every time.

It's easy to get caught up in our own work and consider ourselves a martyr for working so hard pursuing our passion. We are indeed, but we need to remember that our partner may be perfectly happy with us working a "real" j-o-b with all the security, insurance, and paychecks along with it. I left a very lucrative job to publish books making around $2.50 a pop. After twelve months of writing, editing, formatting, and spending money on editors and cover art, I had made a whopping $48.00 on royalties, which didn't even meet the minimum threshold to receive a royalty check. He, on the other hand, was carrying the weight that I wasn't. He would have been more than happy to talk about my day every evening after a full day at a j-o-b. Although he wants to see me happy, he isn't the one feeling the inner turmoil every day that I'm not fulfilling my purpose or chasing my dream. So *not* feeling that wasn't really a benefit to him.

I want to pause for a moment and make sure I am clear that I am by no means suggesting that you put on a full face of makeup every day with a pressed dress and heels and have a hot dinner on the table at six o'clock sharp every evening. This is the 21st century and men can carry their own weight as a participating member of the household. It is not your sole responsibility unless you both discussed and agreed that you would carry the household and somehow carve out time for your pursuing your business. If you were doing the majority of the household chores before, it may be time to re-evaluate the arrangement. If you do not have a supportive family, it may be a little tougher and the balance may be off. The best way to gain your family's support is to start making money. If you just aren't there yet, the next best way is to start treating your business like a business. We talked a bit about this in the mindset section, but it really is so important. How you see your business is how others will begin to see it. If you treat it like a hobby or something you do "when you have time", few people will go out of their way to make sure you have the time to do it. One day we may get there, but most of us aren't there yet.

All of this is just to say, remember the important people in your life and make sure you aren't forgetting them as you pour your heart into your work. Don't forget that having more time with them is a primary reason why you are doing this in the first place. Have a conversation with your spouse and kids, your parents, friends, and anyone else who may miss having you around as much. Let them know what you're doing and make sure they see the light at the end of the tunnel. It will go a long way to gaining and keeping their support.

I want to end this section on a final thought that could use a myth of its own. **Myth:** I tell my husband everything. **Truth:** You don't, and you shouldn't. My niece is learning that "we don't keep secrets". Although I support the idea behind this, there is confusion about what exactly is a secret. If you get a special trip to Chuck E. Cheese, it isn't necessary to come home and tell all of the other kids that didn't get to go about your exciting adventure. In this case, the big reveal is less about "not keeping secrets" and more about rubbing it in that you got to do something awesome and they didn't. We all have things that we don't tell everybody, and when I say "everybody", I mean your spouse. Okay. There. I said it. There are things I don't tell my spouse. Not that it's a secret; it just "didn't come up". It's not always necessary to tell him everything. I didn't tell him that I ate two eggs for lunch or that I spilled coffee on my desk. I didn't tell him that I put on two different socks and then had to find the match. I also didn't tell him that I wanted to throw my computer against the wall and feel like I'll never be successful or that I got rejected by three more agents and feel devastated inside. Again, it just "didn't come up". Now if he asked, I would probably give him some version of that. Just like I wouldn't tell him every detail of the sock incident including that I felt like a moron, blamed him for stealing my sock, or actually found the match under my pillow. I would just tell him what's relevant. It's not a "secret"; it just wasn't necessary detail.

Your spouse wants to protect you, and that includes protecting you from a business that may hurt you. When he asks how your day was and you go on about how terrible it was, how hard it was, how many rejections you received, and how you wonder why you are even doing it, he wants to fix it. His response will naturally be to tell you to stop. Why would you keep doing something that hurts you; that you don't enjoy? Remember, he doesn't get all of the benefits from doing what you love or fulfilling your higher purpose, especially if you don't tell him that. We often jump straight to talking about the hard stuff: the hurt, rejection, and struggle. Instead, I encourage you to talk about the good stuff. Tell your spouse about the victories and what made you feel good. Your spouse wants you to be happy. As long as he knows you are, then he will continue to do everything he can to help you. Once he thinks you aren't, he will start to wonder why he is contributing to your ability to make yourself unhappy.

It's not just the struggle either. Struggle and challenge can be a good thing! It's in how you frame the struggle. Is it bringing you pain or is it exciting and invigorating you? Is it bringing you down or helping you grow? It is all in which side you choose to tell. Now, this is a big one. If you don't see the positive yourself, it will be difficult for you to express the positive to your spouse. Before you even leave your office, I would encourage you to take ten minutes to review your purpose, your challenges, and your day. Take a moment to reframe them in your own mind. Leave your desk with a feeling of accomplishment and pride, and it will be much easier for you to translate that to your spouse. Again, I am not suggesting you "keep secrets" from your spouse or lie to them. I am just suggesting that you choose to tell them only the positive as often as possible. Just like your mom will never forget how your husband made you cry in college, regardless of how many wonderful years you have had since then, your husband will never forget how your business made you feel bad about yourself.

As a psychologist, I encourage people to talk about their feelings. "It's what I do; it's what I *live* for". Little Mermaid? No? I am not suggesting you pretend your struggles and difficulties don't exist. There are days I sit in my office and cry. Entrepreneurship is hard. Like, really hard. It can also feel very isolating and lonely. The first person we want to run to is often our spouse, parent, or even a friend. If those people don't have the same entrepreneurial mindset, they can often, with the best of intentions, completely derail your efforts. I encourage you to find a group of like-minded women and build a network where you can share these struggles with each other. Women who are experiencing the same excitement and struggles will be a much better sounding board than those whose primary mission is to make you feel better. Women with the same mindset will help refocus your attention on your purpose and the meaning behind your work. They will help you find the light at the end of the tunnel and start moving toward it. Rather than turning on your dream, they will inspire you to chase it once again. They will remind you of your mission and rebuild your confidence. *These* are the women you can be completely transparent with.

One day, when your business isn't a tiny baby anymore, you will likely be able to share your deepest fears with your spouse once again. He will have seen your heart and your dedication and will be 100% on board. Perhaps he will even be able to serve the role that these women did in the beginning. If he also has an entrepreneurial mindset or if you have been through similar challenges before, you may reach this point sooner. Your ability to talk about *all* of your feelings as a couple can lead to significant emotional intimacy and strengthen your relationship. When you are able to share your deepest fears and are met with encouragement, you certainly grow as an entrepreneur and a couple. It does not mean that your relationship is broken if you feel that you can't tell your spouse everything right away. Remember that his initial reaction is often to protect you. He doesn't want you hurting and will do everything he can to stop it, including chipping away at your dreams. I would just encourage you to fully assess your own situation before putting all of your cards on the table.

I find myself doing the same thing when the roles are reversed. I don't want to hear all of the bad stuff about my husband's day. I want to hear the good stuff for several reasons. 1.) It's annoying to hear the negative all of the time, 2.) it's really hard for me to stay positive when all I hear is negative, and 3.) if it's so bad, why don't you leave? I don't want to see him hurt by other people, so I want him to get out of there. No sooner do I mention it that I get all of the reasons why he should stay. For him, that was all assumed. He thought I remembered that he loves what he does, has great vacation benefits, and mostly works with really good people. Well no. When all I hear is the negative, why would I assume that the positive still outweighs all of that? I caution you not to assume your spouse will remember all of the positive. Remind them of the good more than the bad. It's okay to tell them the bad sometimes, but there's no need to dwell on it. And certainly, mention the good as often as possible.

Summary:

- Although your family may be super supportive of your dreams, they aren't receiving all of the engagement benefits you are. Make sure they feel your love even while you are in the eye of the storm. Learn about what they need, and do your best to give it to them.

- Get your family involved in reaching big goals. Use your money to pay for a vacation, etc.

- Make sure you tell your spouse and family the good more than the bad

HAPPINESS

Truth 6: Once I get my business off the ground, I will be happy.

Truth 6: Happiness is a *choice.*

What's the deal with "happiness"? Why is it so important? Of all the important things to include in the United States Declaration of Independence, Thomas Jefferson and our forefathers included, "The pursuit of happiness" as one of the unalienable rights alongside life and liberty. "Unalienable" means "not transferable to another or not capable of being taken away or denied".[5] As we were establishing new colonies, saying "goodbye" to family and never seeing them again, we wanted to make sure we preserved the right to pursue our own version of happiness. If it was so important, you would think we would have a better understanding of what it actually is. Although Thomas Jefferson made the phrase famous, a 17th century English Philosopher named John Locke stated that the need to pursue happiness is the foundation upon which liberty is built.[6] He goes on to say that "this pursuit is not merely an imaginary quest or a satisfaction of personal desires, but an ability to achieve the greatest good, free from any predetermined will or forced action". Greek philosophers dating back to the 5th century B.C. defined happiness or "eudaimonia," as individual well-being derived from behaving in alignment with morality, virtue, and utility. They specifically called out that this state is *not* derived from the acquisition of material things. They believed that "peak actualization" is achieved by "living a good life full of positive actions".[6]

Scientists still struggle with clearly defining "happiness". If you type "happiness definition" in the browser Bing, you get the definition "the state of being happy".[7] Talk about descriptive. The Encyclopedia Britannica states that psychologists define happiness as "a state of emotional well-being that a person experiences either in a narrow sense, when good things happen in a specific moment, or more broadly, as a positive evaluation of one's life and accomplishments overall—that is, subjective well-being."[8] As far as a scientific definition of "happiness", this is better than using the word to define itself, but it still doesn't answer the question of whether or not happiness is a temporary state or a lasting trait. As far as society goes, the term gets used to define a temporary state in which it is fluid and can change depending on what's happening at a given time. It has become like the word "love". It has become so misused in our society as we use it to refer to the simplest of emotions. "I *love* this hamburger." "I *love* that shade of pink." Although we may use the term in this sense ourselves, most of us understand that the true meaning of "love" is much more complex and stable over time. I don't love my spouse more on the days he brings home chocolate than I do when he comes home empty-handed. Similarly, happiness has become a state associated with something tangible rather than a more lasting continuous state of being or "trait". When we refer to the lasting, continuous choice to be "happy", Christians often refer to it as "joy". Research in Positive Psychology has attempted to better understand this concept and refer to it as "well-being, of which the temporary state of happiness is one small part. Although we are making strides toward understanding exactly what makes up "happiness" or "well-being", it is still very much remains a mystery that scientists, thousands of years later, are still attempting to understand.

Research shows that the "mood" or state we call happiness is based 40% on genetics, 15% circumstances, and 50% up to us. What this tells us is that the ultimate driving force behind our happiness is *deciding* to be happy. We probably all know those people who are just happy all the time. Personally, they drive me nuts because it highlights just how moody I actually am, but I still oh so want to be just like them. We also know those people who tend to be unhappy in just about every situation. "How was the beach, the party, the dinner?" Regardless, the response is "Meh," or worse yet, a detailed list of everything that was wrong. It is easy to think that it's merely the situation dictating it, but research shows the circumstances account for only 15% of happiness. The reality is, for some people, whether they are at Disney World or scooping poop on a parade route, they just struggle to be happy.

In this sense, happiness or grumpiness is a mood, but when you string enough moods together, it becomes who you are. Once you do this, happiness can move from a state-based mood to a consistent trait or temperament. When someone is "always happy", when it's part of "who they are", we often switch from using the term "happy" to the term "joy". Joy suggests something deeper and more permanent. When someone is filled with the Holy Spirit and reflecting the love of Christ, we believe that should give them a deep sense of joy. If that's the case, why aren't all Christians or Christ-followers described as having joy? And why are some non-believers described as "joyful"? Although being a believer is a great example of a case when someone would be full of joy, it is not automatic. It is still a decision that the individual must make. Connecting to a deeper purpose, such as living for Christ, serves as a great reminder to choose happiness and a foundation for the joy we experience.

Some refer to happiness as a personality trait. "This is just how I am" or "I am happy. This is just how I show it." According to the research above, 40% of it may indeed be personality-, or genetics-based. That said, when we really want to, most of us can behave counter to our personality. I am a natural introvert, but when I am on stage, I have to be outgoing and excited. When I am talking with a group of women, I need to be engaged and engaging. I can't just sit back and read a book, which is what my personality would have me do. When I am in a grumpy mood, I power through it for my children and my family. I put on a smile and crawl around on the floor. Some days I'm better at it than others, but as my friend, Kasey Van Norman once said, "Relationships trump personality." When your family, your business, your friends, or your life calls for it, you show up. If that means adjusting your personality, then, by all means, put on a smile and change the outward demonstration of your personality. This is where the phrase "fake it 'til you make it" comes into play as well. This is based on the idea that if you do it enough times, it becomes a habit, which then becomes part of who you are. Remember that your brain does not differentiate between reality and what you tell it. If you tell yourself you a pleasant person enough times by "pretending" to be a positive person, eventually your brain will start to believe you truly are.

I'm not suggesting you change who you are. Well, I might be suggesting that on a small scale, but I do believe we attribute far too much to "personality". I don't feel like it...personality. I don't like it....personality. It's too much work....personality. In reality, we have given ourselves permission to slack and take the easy way out far too often. When someone is rude to someone else in the name of "honesty", they say "That's just the way I am". When "the way you are" is hurtful to someone else, then yes, you need to change. And if your potentially self-created personality is holding you back from reaching your goals or connecting with your family, then by all means, change it. Don't be so prideful or stuck in your ways to think you can't or shouldn't change. Your life situations, choices you've made, and people in your life have helped form the personality or "mood" you find yourself displaying most often. It has become a habit, your natural default. Don't stick to it out of pride or stubbornness. I encourage you to recognize where your behaviors and responses aren't serving you or those around you and open yourself up to making an adjustment. We all need tweaks from time to time. Heck, I have a line of edits I'm working on. It's just the way life is. We learn, and we change. Don't let this area be a downfall for you.

So if we shape our happiness, how do we do that? Research in the relatively young field of Positive Psychology has revealed that happiness or wellbeing is comprised of several components: positive emotion / pleasure (the state of feeling good), engagement (being completely absorbed in your work), relationships (being authentically connected to others), meaning (purposeful existence), and achievement (a sense of accomplishment and success). It's no surprise that these factors sound a lot like those we discussed earlier under engagement: meaning, autonomy, growth, impact, and connection. What is surprising is that positive emotion, which is what we often refer to as "happiness", has no impact on overall wellbeing unless the other components (engagement, relationships, meaning, and achievement) are experienced as well. Dr. Martin Seligman, one of the fathers of positive psychology, describes positive emotion as "Hollywood happiness". This idea comes from the seemingly happy celebrities who are all smiles in front of the camera or while partying through the night. According to Seligman, this outward expression of happiness or positive emotion is simply the cherry on the top of the happiness sundae. In reality, it contributes very little to the actual experience of being "happy".

Although all of the factors discussed contribute to the overall experience of happiness, there are two that have the greatest impact: engagement and meaning. I discuss the importance of these two factors throughout this book because they are so incredibly powerful. Many authors discuss the role of meaning as the driving force of your behavior. When you live and work with purpose, your behaviors are guided by a greater sense of urgency and you find greater fulfillment in your life. As I mentioned earlier, circumstances account for only 15% of your happiness. When you are driven with purpose, the situation doesn't control you. When I was going through a rough patch in my career, I would wake up with the goal of being happy. Inevitably, someone would do something and my mood would shift. I realized I was being dictated by the situation. In fact, I was preparing for and mentally rehearsing the annoyances before they even happened. Eventually, I was *un*happy regardless of the situation. When I started living by a higher purpose, I stopped allowing these annoyances to dictate my mood. It's not perfect, but for the most part, bumps are just part of the greater mission in front of me. I choose to be happy because my mission depends on it. When you are aligned with a greater sense of purpose, you are not driven by circumstances. Rather, your experience of the world around you is dictated by your internal state of well-being.

In positive psychology's theory of well-being, the definition of engagement is a bit different than the one we discussed in the last few sections. In the organizational setting, we often use the term engagement to refer to a deep sense of connection or belonging, aligning with a greater purpose, and being deeply involved in your work and the organization. This definition is more along the lines of positive psychology's definition of "meaning", which represents a sense of connection and purpose rather than the experience of "flow".

In terms of factors contributing to happiness or well-being, the definition of engagement is more specific and refers to the act of being completely absorbed in your work. In the opening of this book, I touched briefly on the concept of flow. This is when you are so engaged in your work that time stands still. Have you ever been working on a project and you realize that you've been at it for hours? Your back is sore, your throat is dry, and you have no idea where your kids are? Hopefully, someone else is watching them, but you haven't even heard a peep. I used to get like this when I would scrapbook. I could be up all night just snipping and thinking and gluing. Time passed, but I wasn't aware of it. Time would move from 9:20 to 10:45 to 12:10 in what felt like minutes.

Time can also seem to stand still. Laser-sharp focus during flow can result in seemingly impossible amounts of productivity in a very short amount of time. I knocked out an entire chapter and looked at the clock thinking it would be time for lunch. Only thirty-five minutes had passed since I started working. Other times it takes me a few hours to compose a solid chapter. I was also in that state when I was writing my first book. I was so deeply engaged with my thoughts that nothing else broke through. Science has shown that your brain waves actually slow down mirroring deep meditation, a trance-like state, or even that state right before you fall asleep when ideas flow freely and uninhibited. When you are *this* engaged in your work, you can have incredible insight and output. When you experience flow in your work, you have a deep sense of satisfaction, accomplishment, and elation.

When I was writing my book, I just couldn't wait to get back to it. I would gobble up food hand-delivered by my incredible husband and dive back into my work. There is almost an addictive draw to being back in that state. Being in a state of flow causes the brain to release larger quantities of norepinephrine, dopamine, endorphins, anandamide, and serotonin. All of these neurochemicals are pleasure-inducing and performance-enhancing. Norepinephrine and dopamine amp up focus, boosting imaginative possibilities by helping us gather more information, increasing pattern recognition, and increasing our ability to link ideas together in new ways. Anandamide increases lateral thinking, expanding the size of the database searched by the pattern recognition system. This is the difference in having ideas flow freely, seeing connections easily, and thinking faster than you can get the words on paper. When you experience writer's block and you can't even hack ideas out with a pick-ax, you are likely low on these neurochemicals. A brisk walk or sweat session can also help jump-start the creative process by boosting these chemicals.

Take a moment to think about a time when you found yourself in a deep state of flow. What were you doing? What did it feel like? What were some of the contributing factors to getting you into that state? How did it make you feel? Answering these questions will help shine a light on some of the activities that give you the greatest satisfaction, engagement, and ultimately lead to happiness for you.

In addition to finding what gives you meaning and engagement, there are other things you can do to increase your overall happiness or well-being. I mentioned that during flow, your brain waves resemble the waves during deep meditation or a trance-like state. When studied from the angle of meditation, researchers find similar feelings of happiness and wellbeing during and after meditation. Through even short spurts of meditation such as five or fifteen minutes, you can experience the same benefits of flow. Meditation, which is essentially focusing on a single thought or no thought at all, forces you to live only in the moment. By bringing your attention to right now, you fully experience the world within you. During flow, you are focused on a singular task or activity. You release the worry, stress, and anxiety that often accompany our thought and activity. During this time, your brain has the opportunity to rest and release positive, healing hormones.

Another way to improve your happiness is through your environment. Who you hang out with has a significant impact on how you see the world around you and your ultimate happiness or enjoyment in life. Research shows that unhappiness[9] and loneliness[10] are contagious. Not only do you have a significant impact on the people around you, but they have a significant impact on you. Scientific research is revealing an energy force that each of us has. This energy is all connected. Feelings are quickly and directly spread through this energy field to those around you. Have you ever walked into a room and just gotten a bad feeling? Some of us are more perceptive of this energy field than others, but it doesn't mean we are immune to its influence. Be careful who you hang out with and who you let hang around your family. They have a greater impact on your overall life satisfaction than you may think or want to believe. Even if you don't quite buy into the research on energy, research shows that employees who sat within a twenty-five-foot radius of high-performers showed a 15% increase in performance, which amounted to a one-million-dollar improvement to the bottom line. Unfortunately, the negative impact on employees sitting near low-performers could have double the impact of the high-performer influence, just in the wrong direction.[11] Although this research is set in the work environment, we have every reason to believe this study could be replicated in the school, home, or small business setting. There is a saying that you are most like the five people you spend the most time with. Behavior and energy are contagious. Establishing a culture that draws those who share your values and beliefs will have a profound impact on maintaining that culture within your family or small business.

The environment also plays a significant role in entering and maintaining a state of flow. It is important to get yourself set up for a state of flow. For some, this is getting comfortable. For others, this is getting fully dressed in their *work* mode. For me, when I am in my creative space, I need to be super comfortable. When I am working on a number of tasks, I need to be fully dressed for the day, getting my mindset right for work. Getting dressed allows you to mentally be in work mode. Your subconscious brain is triggered to start waking up and get those neurons ready to fire. When you wear jammies all day, your brain loses an important cue for what it should be doing. Am I waking up or getting ready for bed? Not only does this create difficulty focusing during work hours, but it can interfere with your ability to wind down at the end of the night. As much as I love wearing my slippers and comfortable pants, I find that I work much better when I am dressed for the task at hand.

Distractions are plentiful in your home environment. Not only do we have the distractions of our emails, texts, and notifications, but we also have the distractions that go along with being at home: laundry needs done, dishes are piled up, the toilet is running, the kids need lunch. If you don't keep your house or workspace clutter-free (like me), then that is yet another contender for your attention. In order to be most effective at your work, it is critical to clear out the clutter: mentally and physically. Remove all of the papers, books, and mail stacked up on your desk, finish or get rid of those unfinished projects and crafts that are sitting around in boxes, turn off all notifications and web browsers, and move as far as possible from other people in the house. It is almost impossible to enter flow with your brain darting in 100 different directions.

Within organizations, we focus quite a bit of energy trying to eliminate external distractions, and this really isn't anything new. In 1925, Hugo Gernsback created The Isolator. It was an invention intended to combat office distractions. It looked somewhat like a big metal space helmet and was intended to help keep employees focused on their work; kind of like blinders for a horse. The Isolator did indeed serve its purpose of reducing external distractions in the workplace. Unfortunately, it did not serve the function of keeping employees focused on their work. I can't imagine that employees struggled to work with a metal bucket on their heads, but what Gernsback discovered was that 50% of distractions actually came from within. If 50% of distractions came from within the employees themselves in 1925 with no social media, no internet, no computers, and significantly less information coming at them, how much greater might that number would be now that our attention spans are even shorter. It was said that a wealth of information creates a poverty of attention. This continuous distraction, whether from within ourselves or from the world around us, makes it increasingly difficult to cultivate a life of focus. If you want to make a true impact and move the needle in your life, it is critical to develop the ability to eliminate internal distractions.

Summary:

- Happiness is a choice.

- Meaning and engagement are more important to happiness than positive emotion (what feels good).

- Your environment has a significant impact on your ability to enter flow, which is critical for creativity.

CULTURE

Myth 7: Establishing a culture is only for big business.

Truth 7: Any grouping of individuals can have an associated culture, and it makes a difference.

Organizations love culture. They don't always do it well, but most organizations have a culture that others can see and feel. When you think about Google, Amazon, and Facebook, what things come to mind? Young, bring your dog to work, open communication, flat reporting structures, and ping pong tables come to mind for me. When you think about organizations like Walmart, Lowe's, and The Home Depot, what comes to mind? Good old boy, multiple layers, business casual, and bureaucracy come to mind for me. Now that's not entirely fair or accurate, but every organization has a culture. Your small business has a culture, your side hustle has a culture, and your family has a culture.

Despite the reality that every grouping has one, we rarely stop to ask "What is my culture?" Not what you *want* it to be, but what it actually is? Organizations often overlook this and let it develop on its own for years, or it is driven by the founder. Often times, when the founder leaves the organization, and the primary driver of the culture is no longer active, it begins to crumble. It isn't until stocks begin to fall that the company pulls out all the stops and looks into this culture nonsense. Consulting organizations are often called in to examine the culture from an outside perspective. It is time-consuming, and it is not cheap. You may be asking why organizations put in so much time and effort to change their cultures. And this is a great question. In fact, many organizations still have not bought into the whole "culture thing" either. Those that do, though, experience a number of benefits that have others wondering what they are doing so right.

First of all, organizations with strong cultures retain, attract, and get the most out of their employees in terms of productivity. The ability to retain talent is crucial to organizational success. Not only do you lose valuable information with each employee that walks out the door, but it can cost 30% to 200% or more of an employee's salary just to bring them on board! That doesn't even include the cost of training, ramp up, and downtime caused by having an empty seat during the search process. It is very expensive to hire someone and get them up to speed. If they are not a good fit with your culture, they may leave before they have even had a chance to start producing any return at all.

A strong organizational culture also helps attract employees whose values naturally align with yours. This could be an alignment of work style or an alignment of purpose. Either way, these employees are more likely to seek your organization out. Having an available candidate pipeline to fill your roles is invaluable to the hiring process. Finally, employees who support their organization's culture work harder for them. They are more productive and the organizations are more profitable than those without strong cultures. You don't have to be a multi-billion-dollar corporation to understand and change your culture, and you don't have to be a large organization to experience these benefits either. Although they may look slightly different if you are developing your family culture versus your business culture, you can still experience the benefits of a strong culture. I will walk you through the process, and you can start reaping the benefits of having a culture aligned with your values and objectives.

Culture is a major driving force for success. An organization's culture is how they align marketing, branding, and major organizational decisions. Each organization has a different culture. Take the cultures of Amazon versus the culture of a mom and pop shop. Take the culture of Google versus Walmart. The organizational culture determines the type of people who will be attracted to work at the organization and ultimately, those who will thrive. When the culture doesn't align with the individual's expectations or goals, the misalignment causes a great deal of frustration for both the organization and the employee.

I have worked for many organizations who have tried to change their culture. It is a painful and long process. Why is that? An organization's culture is made up of their joint experiences, values, and beliefs. It drives everything from the products they promote to the way they dress. It is a major part of how the organization operates. Family cultures are very similar. When cultures develop unintentionally, they can go in a direction that the organization, or the family, doesn't want. Before they know it, the culture has become something different than what they want.

Summary:

- Any group of people can have a culture, including your family and/or small business.

- The benefits of a strong culture include retaining, attracting, and getting the most out of your employees.

- These benefits extend to families and small businesses as well, though they may look a little different.

CULTIVATING CULTURE

Myth 8: I know my family culture.

Truth 8: Sometimes what we *think* our culture is and what it *actually* is are two different things.

The first step in establishing an effective culture is to understand your current culture. What are the experiences, beliefs, and values that you are instilling in your children with your language, activities, and what you allow? How do you operate your business or manage yourself? You may say you value certain things, but are you living them? Are the behaviors you are displaying and rewarding in alignment with what you want your culture to be?

I had an idea about what my family culture was, but it was based entirely on what I always thought it would be. I always imagined my family culture would be warm, loving, calm, open and honest, healthy, family-oriented, have a sense of humor, active, frugal, fiscally conservative, and driven. When I actually stopped and evaluated it, it was not at all what I thought it was. Based on my own behaviors and language, it turned out I was cultivating a culture that was sarcastic, passive-aggressive, angry, lazy, built around fast food, debt, and plain boring. Some of the areas were still spot on. I could definitely tell which parts of the culture were most important to me. Anyone looking from the outside could tell that family was the top priority, often at the expense of something else. No cost was too high for family. We would pay for vacations, buy a bigger house than we could afford so we could support our extended family if needed and have a nice place to gather, we would take family out and travel to see them, even when we didn't have the time or money to do it. Although family is very important, we didn't take into consideration all aspects of our culture and how it was impacting it. What were we teaching our kids about finances and sacrifice? Is the message they were receiving the same message we thought we were sending out?

I focus so much on family culture here because small business and entrepreneurship often revolve around the family. You often work from home, your kids and spouse are involved in the business, and you work long into the night. The business culture affects the family and the family culture affects the business. Just like Walmart took on the culture of its founder Sam Walton, your small business will take on the culture you set. Your values, beliefs, and past experiences. By addressing your family culture, we can tackle two critical areas at once. I like to say, "My family *is* my business. It's all family business."

So let's start breaking it down. Taking a good, hard look at your culture requires you to take a look at your behaviors, thoughts, experiences, words, and attitude. How do you handle conflict? How do you discipline? How do you respond when things don't turn out the way you had planned? How long did you plan your last vacation? What do you spend your money, time, and resources on? Given a free weekend, what do you spend your time doing? Answering these questions will give you some insight into your personal and family values. Often, people's values change once they have a family. Although they feel this internally, it often doesn't translate to actions.

The second step in establishing the culture you want is to define what you want your culture to be. What are the values, beliefs, and experiences you want for you, your spouse, your children? What are the core values, what is your mission statement, what are the core competencies that you can promote to support that culture? Cultivating a culture that you *want* does not happen by itself. You must be active and present in creating that culture. Otherwise, you may wake up and find out that it is not what you expected. Previous to my entry into the workforce, large organizations tended to continue operating as they always had. It was acceptable to respond with "because that's how we've always done it" when confronted with the question of why we were doing something a certain way. Shortly after, a major trend moved through organizations to stop allowing bad behavior or practices. "Because that's how we've always done it" became an unacceptable reason for doing something.

In the early 2000s, there began a shift in that thinking. No longer were unhealthy behaviors tolerated just because they have served us well for 30, 50, or 100 years. The world was evolving, and organizations began to slowly catch on. It became acceptable to question old patterns of behavior and call out "in a rut" thinking. This was the beginning of significant organizational culture change across America. But it wasn't enough to just say, "We want to change". Organizations needed a vision for where they wanted to be in the next fifty years. They began to understand the importance of the beliefs they held, the language they used, and the behaviors they accepted. Thus began a significant movement toward organizational culture change.

When designing the culture you want, forget about the current culture. Forget about the person you think you've always been, the ways you've always acted, and the way you've allowed others to treat you. Set all of that aside and image the person you want to be, the family environment you want to foster, and the business you want to have. What are the behaviors, beliefs, actions, and language associated with that image?

I grew up repeating the self-belief that I never finished anything. I carried that with me into adulthood, and it's almost a running joke. "There goes Cheryl again, starting something she won't finish." Even if people didn't say it, *I* said it. Every time I shared a new idea, I imagined my family rolling their eyes and. I felt the need to explain myself and how "this time was different", even when no one asked. Inevitably, I would fulfill my own prophecy that I didn't finish what I started. It became a part of who I thought I was and ultimately became part of the culture I passed onto my family and business. Just because you have been a certain way for more than a decade, that doesn't mean you have to continue to be that way. You can start changing your culture right now, but you must know where you want to go.

In addition to outlining the characteristics of the culture you want, there are some additional components that can serve to align all of your team members or family members to the culture. Your culture is based on the set of beliefs and values you (collectively) hold. Therefore, the first step to defining your culture is to understand what those beliefs and values are. Beliefs and values are like your central operating system. All of your behaviors, responses, activities, and decisions are linked to that system. It is important to intentionally set up those values. That operating system is always running in the background whether you are directing it or not. So take some time to really define the values that are driving your decisions behind the scenes. Below are some questions to get you started:

What are your basic beliefs about yourself?

What are your basic beliefs about your future?

What are your beliefs about your purpose in life?

What are your core values; the values by which you live and behave?

What is important to you?

What characteristics would you like your kids, spouse, and employees to demonstrate?

Is your message clear across all areas or are there inconsistencies? Identify clusters of similar traits. Patterns should begin to emerge to give you a good picture of the foundation for your culture. Some organizations stop here. They begin making posters and promoting their values on their website. Some even start instructing their recruiters to look for employees that embody these values. Unfortunately, values don't always say the same thing to different people. In industrial-organizational psychology, we define *everything* with behaviors. If a definition is good, behavioral examples are better. We even have an entire rating system based on behaviors called BARS – Behaviorally Anchored Rating Scale. Once you start defining expectations based on behaviors, you never go back!

If you really want your values to be understood and adopted, which you do, then you must define the behaviors associated with that value. What does it *mean* to be creative? What does it *mean* to be faithful? What does it *mean* to be present? I have a friend whose family lives by the values: Be honest. Be silly. Be kind. They repeat it every day in their home and have it on the wall. Being honest, I get, but my family isn't really silly. That may not resonate with me. What exactly does it mean to be silly? Now the parents don't need to necessarily sit down with their kids and outline what being silly means, but they should have a pretty solid idea of what is acceptable and what is not. As they live their lives, the acceptable behaviors are rewarded and celebrated while the offending behaviors are not. This gives the children direction, boundaries, and a sense of security. When children (and employees) know what to expect, what behaviors are acceptable or unacceptable, they develop trust and are more likely to try new things. They know where the line is and aren't afraid of accidentally crossing it. They may, and probably will push the limits, but through a consistent response, children learn to live within the boundaries and have a much better sense of safety and trust.

If the parents are not 100% in alignment with their definitions of silliness, they may find themselves rewarding and punishing conflicting behaviors. This creates a culture of confusion and insecurity. Eventually, the kids will learn to behave differently around their parents and will be in an uncomfortable state of limbo when both parents are together. This same logic translates within organizations. Executive leadership will often promote a set of values and may even define clear behavioral expectations. When middle management disagrees or disregards them, it creates a terrible situation for the employees who are stuck in the middle between two feuding "parents".

Back to the behaviors aligned with values. These behaviors will give you a blueprint for how you talk and interact with each other and what behaviors you decide are okay. When I worked for Walmart, they had a sundown policy. This means that you responded to every email, phone call, or message you received that day before the "sun goes down". This often meant we were working long into the evening to make sure we got it done, but we responded to every message even if it was to say, "I received your message and will get back with you tomorrow." I didn't realize how critical that one rule was. It showed a sense of respect for each other that I lost in other organizations. So often I would allow myself to be passive-aggressive to others by withholding a response. Sometimes it's the only way you can "get back" at someone who you feel has wronged you, and we did indeed use it in that way. There would be week-long "email wars" in which we would not respond or not respond completely. Can you imagine what that does to a team or an organization? That one simple rule was so much more than a rule. It demonstrated a sense of respect for each other that was lost in other organizations. That one "rule" or "policy" was instrumental in the culture.

It's also critical that the behaviors you reward and those you discipline are in alignment with those values. Innovation is one of those values that is especially popular right now. Every organization thinks they need to incorporate innovation as a core value. Unfortunately, not all organizations really understand what that means. True innovation requires a certain amount of vulnerability and risk-taking. When employees try and fail, the value of innovation suggests that leadership would be supportive of the employee. Leaders would see the attempt as a learning experience and encourage the employee to identify what went wrong and try again. Asking questions, brainstorming, and trying new things are encouraged and supported in an innovative culture. Many leaders struggle with this change. They remain risk-averse rather than risk managing. The first time an employee is fired for a project failing when the risks were calculated and prepared for, the culture/value alignment begins to break down. When you are attempting to promote specific values within your family or business, it is critical to understand exactly what is involved in each value. Define the associated behaviors and make sure all parties are in alignment. Early on, mistakes are expected. As you establish a culture of honesty and forgiveness, this can serve as a great opportunity to discuss those values, the mistakes, and establish a precedent for the response. Your family will begin to see the connection and your sincerity behind the values.

Values also serve another purpose within organizations. Research clearly shows that employees are most satisfied when they feel they are part of a greater purpose. When we can align the work they are doing with greater organizational objectives, they have a sense of direction. But when we can align the work they do with a greater purpose beyond making money for an organization, they have a sense of meaning. We talked about the importance of *meaning* and its role in well-being and engagement earlier in this book, but I wanted to tie it back to this discussion of values. When an employee or family member is aligned with those values, they have a greater sense of purpose. Their work is no longer about the product but about the bigger picture. In that sense, adhering to a strong set of values can ultimately lead to greater happiness as well.

A myth related to this discussion that organizations often get themselves caught up with is that getting results is all that matters. In reality, when you lose sight of *how* you get the results, eventually, the results don't matter. It sounds like a no-brainer, and it would be easy to think this myth applies only to big business, but this myth can creep up on your small business as well. We may not have the analysts criticizing our progress or a board of directors evaluating our purchases, but we do have children and families watching our every move. Integrity is a little word with a huge impact. I would go out on a limb to say it's even more important in our family businesses than in the corporate world.

Integrity displays itself when things are tough. What decisions do you make when no one is looking or when the consequences of doing the right thing are high? Organizations that set values and use those values to drive every decision they make are said to have high integrity. It is when decision-makers drift from those values and think, "this one time won't matter" that the breakdown begins. This is said to happen quite a bit when the founders of an organization leave. They have set the standards, but as soon as they are gone, the values begin to degrade.

We talked earlier about the change management process and the importance of transformational change when it comes to matters of values. It is critical for leaders in the organization to really understand and buy into the organizational values. If not, when the figurehead driving the values is gone, they will indeed break down. This idea transcends business and is clear in families and small businesses.

Summary:

- Families and small businesses have a culture and it may not be what you expect.

- To change your culture, you must evaluate your culture to determine if you have established the culture you want.

- Establish values to support your culture. They must have a definition and behavioral examples to be effective.

SUCCESS

Myth 9: My success is determined by the amount of money I make.

Truth 9: God's version of success and yours may be different.

Success. What a strange little word with such vast meaning. Most of my life, I defined success as I believe so many do. It all revolved around money, achievement, and status. "Go to college so you can get a good job with a good income." "Work hard so you can get promoted and get a bigger paycheck." "You may not like your job, but it is secure." For most of my life, I defined my own success by how much money I was making. By that definition, I was pretty successful. I also defined it by what I could do for myself with that money. I could take my extended family on trips and pick up the tab when we went out. I could buy whatever Facebook Ad flickered across my screen, and I could start a new adventure for the sheer purpose of "trying it" because I had the extra cash flow. If my car broke down, I could fix it. If my teeth were a little crooked, I could adjust them. If I wanted to quit my job and try something else, I could do it. Money does allow you certain freedoms, so it's no wonder it has so deeply become our definition of success.

Success also comes in the form of outward validation. When I was writing my first book, I didn't care if I sold a single copy. I was doing it because writing a book had always been a dream of mine. *writing* a book; not *selling* a book. Of course, once I wrote it and published it, I sure did watch my reports to see if anyone was buying it. Suddenly I craved the validation that came with someone purchasing it. I craved the validation that said, "You're a writer". I craved the life that I imagined being a writer might provide. When I really stopped to think about my definition of success, I realized that it was all about the outcome; the outward validation.

My parents owned a small t-shirt printing business for almost twenty-five years. I was sweeping the floor on my last day in town before moving several states away to graduate school. I remember sweeping and thinking how disappointed they must be that their business wasn't more successful. Although our business did not break any records, it gave us a life that few others had.

In high school and through college, I was in every marching and concert band that was offered. We had performances all the time, and my parents never missed a single one, including traveling across the state in the middle of the day. We also traveled and experienced more than most of the kids I grew up with. Most importantly to me, we were together All. The. Time. My brothers and I worked with my parents in the sales and production offices throughout the summer, during school breaks, and after school. We had lunch together every day. When a significant project was due, we all pulled together and got it done. We knew the value of money because we watched the bank account drop and then experienced the excitement when a payment finally came through to cover the bills. I learned how to be an entrepreneur by learning how to be a good employee first. I learned more in that small business than I could have ever learned by watching them go to work anywhere else. It allowed my parents to impact the lives of others through their service. It helped us grow as a family. Although the business may not have developed into what they or anyone else initially that it would, by looking through a different lens, it was more successful than they ever could have imagined.

I encourage you to take a moment to as yourself that question. What does success mean to you? Said another way, what would it take for you to stop, give up, or set aside your dream? For many, it's having enough money to buy and do the things they want. It may also be that outward validation of success, status, approval, and acceptance by others. I used to watch a show about people who moved into these tiny houses that could be pulled or hauled by a truck. On one of the promotional videos for the show, a guy is lying in a hammock on his deck reading a book. The voiceover says, "We are redefining what success looks like." My first thought was, "No you aren't. Success still requires achievement." But maybe it doesn't. It's about living on your terms. Once defined by how much stuff you can buy or what you can do, now it's about seeing the world and answering to yourself. One day we were talking about the family business and my mom said she wished it had been more successful. I said, "Mom, it was incredibly successful. It gave us time."

When I think about the impact my choices have on my life and the lives of my children, it is about so much more than money or even the lifestyle I think it will give me. My definition of success has evolved to mean more than that. Success is knowing that I am living up to my potential and following my heart. It's about fulfilling God's purpose in my life, wherever it may lead me and whatever it may look like. It's about living on my own terms and based on my own values. Before you start a new venture, or if you already have, take a moment to pause and think about your definition of success. Why are you doing your business or side-hustle? What would need to happen for you to feel successful? How much would it need to produce to be a viable business for you? These numbers may be different than what you *hope* or would like for it to become, but the numbers should not be mixed. Don't believe that your business is not successful just because it may not (yet) be where you want it to be.

I do believe that your business will be prosperous if you are following your God-given purpose. Although it doesn't always manifest in making a dump truck full of money, it will indeed prosper. I used to have a sign on my desk at work that said, "What would you do if you knew you would not fail?" I used to stare at that sign and think, "One day I'll make the leap. One day I will leave this ball and chain to pursue my life's purpose. Once I do, I will be unstoppable!" The thought of failure held me back for years. Sure, if I knew it would be wildly successful, I'd have jumped ship long ago. But for me, failure meant that it wouldn't take off, that it wouldn't be able to replace my income, and that I wouldn't be able to pay my bills (i.e., have the luxuries that I was accustomed to). The idea of not being successful by my own definition held me back from even trying. I didn't have to quit my job to do it, but for me, success was doing it full time, the grand gesture. I completely overlooked the whispers that said, "I've got this. Just do what I'm asking you to do. Right here. Right now." Now, I would like to change that sign to read, "What would you do if you knew God's definition of success was different than your own?" When we dream about our life one day, it usually does involve an idea of money. I encourage you to explore a broader definition of success. When you are writing on a specific outcome to feel successful, there is a good chance you will never get there. When the journey *is* the outcome, you are successful merely by taking one step at a time. The mere act of doing becomes the definition of success.

As I pursue my dream now, I am taken aback by my previously narrow view of success. Money, achievement, and validation just cannot compare to following God's purpose for your life. When your head and heart are in alignment with that purpose, the things that mattered before don't matter anymore. Yes, money is important; you need money. Once you step into who you were made to be, you can see beyond the bills. I went through a rough patch between contracts, and I just couldn't find any work. I was writing and speaking for free, but my bill-paying j-o-b wasn't coming through for me. It was during that time that I got serious and looked to God. As our savings account began to drain, I said, "God, I thought you were going to take care of us. I trust you, but we are running out of money, and nothing is coming through. I know you have a plan for me, but how can I fulfill that plan if I can't pay my bills?"

I had been putting off my purpose for more than two decades at this point. I was working lucrative but unfulfilling j-o-bs. I just knew I had a greater purpose that I was ignoring. As much as I knew that, I didn't act on it. I just sat in my not-so comfort zone. In my struggle, I heard God clearly respond, "Cheryl, don't you know that my plans are bigger than your bills? I have you, but I am working on something bigger than this." I also heard him clearly say, "When you had that nice, cushy job I gave you, you didn't do what I asked you to do. I have just removed all of your distractions so you can focus." I tried bartering with God by showing Him that I could work and write at the same time, but deep down, I knew He had something bigger for me in mind. During that time, He really spoke to me about what success looked like to Him. As I told Him my deepest desires for success, I began to hear whispers pointing me to HIS definition of success. It finally came to a shout in the form of coffee with our church's women's minister. For some reason, she told me a story about another staff member. At seminary, he asked his philosophy professor, "What does a successful life in Christ look like?" The professor thought about it for a moment while the class anticipated a deep, inspirational speech about success.

After a moment the professor responded, "Just be faithful."

Sometimes, I think we get so wrapped up in our own goals that we lose sight of why we are really here. When I did finally look to God for guidance, I was paralyzed by fear of messing up. I didn't want to say the wrong thing, do the wrong thing, or not quite hit what God had in mind. I was so afraid of doing it wrong that I didn't do anything at all. When I looked at God's plan for me through this lens, I realized that everything else was secondary. Success in Christ is obedience; being faithful.

God expects big things from us. There is no doubt about that. But it brings me such peace to know that the biggest thing He expects of me is to simply follow Him. To actually *do* what He has called me to do. There isn't a certain amount of money He expects me to make or a certain number of people I'm supposed to talk to. His plan is so much bigger than anything I can imagine. If I don't hear back from event planners, I feel like I have failed. I feel like I have let God down because I haven't booked a gig. I didn't hit my goals, I didn't have a big enough impact, and I am not living up to my purpose. When I start getting down on myself, I hear God say, "Whoa! Slow your roll. I know what I'm doing. Trust me. Know that I have this under control. Believe it or not, *this is* part of my plan. *This is* your purpose. It will all happen in my time." We don't know what He is doing behind the scenes. By doing the work, we learn valuable lessons to help us down the road. By starting small, we are better able to handle the big. By growing where we are planted, we are gaining the skills and experience needed for the work He has planned for us down the road. My grandmother has the best sayings. One of my favorites is, "No experience is wasted." At ninety-seven years old, she still jumps at the opportunity to try something new. She doesn't recognize us anymore, yet she will engage for as long as we visit with her. Oh to have that mentality that no experience, no conversation, no moment is wasted. How much more could we learn from life if we went into every day with that perspective?

Make sure that you and God are using the same measuring stick. In business, we have KPIs or key performance indicators that tell us how we are performing with a given project. How's it going? We both need to know what the measure of success is. I was working with a vendor on a selection project. As the project rolled on, we realized that we had two different ideas of success. Their idea of success was to design the scoring so that a smaller number of clearly superior candidates were at the top of the list. That way, there were only a few candidates to bring in and move along through the process. As far as they were concerned, the project was successful because only four candidates for a specific job were moved through the process. Our hiring manager blew a gasket because they only had four candidates from which to choose three to interview. In his mind, the program was successful if it simply weeded out the bottom performers so that he had more candidates to review and bring in for an interview. Their definitions of success were very different. As the professional brought in to sort the whole thing out, either would have been okay, though the vendor's version made me a lot happier. It was my job to sit down and help guide the conversation and come to a resolution. As a professional, I encourage you to take some time to understand what faithfulness looks like for you. What is God calling you to do to advance His kingdom? How might your idea of success differ from His, and how might that interfere with your willingness to be faithful? Knowing that obedience is the stick by which God measures our faithfulness, what impact might that have on your actions and the way you feel about success? How might this keep you from getting discouraged when things aren't going as you imagined they would? What would you attempt if you knew God's definition of success was based on your faithfulness?

Although faithfulness is the primary indicator of success in Christ, He does not expect us to walk around eating bugs. We do need to pay our bills, feed our children, have a savings account, and take some time to rest. I have a friend and mentor who once said she was on the Manna Plan. God was providing her with just what she needed when she needed it. Although we have certain obligations, there are areas where we can likely cut down. We don't need a new Kate Spade purse every time the 75% off flash sale pops up. We also don't need a matching bra and panty subscription each month. As you pursue your dreams and purpose with all you have, there may be some things that you need to live without for a season. For me, this was very hard. I had to give up the security of knowing that I could repair my car with cash whenever it broke down, purchasing the latest gadget I saw advertised, even if it would completely change my life, and going out to eat just because I forgot to thaw out some chicken. I had to put my trust in God, but I also had to do my part to get rid of some of the extra luxuries that were keeping me tethered to a job that did not satisfy me and a life without purpose (outside of my family, of course).

At this time, I encourage you to take a moment to think about what you would be willing to sacrifice to live the life that you want. When I initially planned on leaving my job and following my passion, I thought I had to replace my income. What a silly idea. For one thing, I won't be replacing my income for a while, but also, I was paying a huge price to myself for doing something I didn't love. I was frustrated and agitated, my insides were tangled, and every day, I sat at my desk knowing that I was not where I was supposed to be. That alone was majorly costly. I took a good look at what I would be gaining by doing what I loved. Not only in terms of money and feeling better, but the driving force behind a change was to be the mom I always wanted to be and to be the wife that my husband deserved. I wanted to do those things with my family that led me to have a family in the first place. You can't put a price on that, but if you could, that would be another "benefit" that adds to your total compensation package.

The formula for "successful", which is really just the amount we need to sustain the business in order to keep doing it and have the lifestyle we want, is:

$$[(Income + Lifestyle) - What\ You\ Can\ Live\ Without]$$

Income represents the income from your business. This must be added to the lifestyle or extra perks that having your own business affords you. There is certainly freedom that comes with having your own business as well as the joy that comes from doing what you know you are called to do. These are lifestyle benefits that must be added to the income to capture the complete picture of what you are gaining in your business. Then, you must subtract when you can actually live without. In order to enjoy those benefits and perks of having your own business. Although you may be enjoying a certain lifestyle right now because you can afford them and need to drown the pain of selling your soul, when you are living the life of your dreams, you may not need those things. Which is good, because you probably won't be able to afford them for a while.

It's silly to think that I can quit one job I've been doing for a decade, step into something I've been only thinking about, and pull the same income. In order to make the leap, I needed to think about those things that I would need to give up to really give myself a fighting chance. I was gaining so many things, but I would also be losing some. This is where you can really cut back to make following your passion even more feasible. This includes things like cable television, eating out frequently, choice of restaurants, type and frequency of travel, having the ability to pay for car repairs in full, a padded savings account, making significant contributions to retirement, surplus toys for kids, donations to charity, etc.

The reduction of these things is often what leads people to believe they are not successful. It feels scary, it's uncomfortable, and it's different. From the outside, it looks like you are doing without and struggling, so something must be wrong. It's critical, though, to also closely evaluate what you have gained through your change. When the cost outweighs the benefit, you either hunker down and push through and see what changes you can make or reconsider whether or not this is the right time to follow your passion. As mentioned previously, this can be a significant change for the entire family. If they are not on board, the sacrifices can become too much for them. It is important for them to understand their role and believe that you are indeed committed to making the sacrifice period as short as possible.

Summary:

- The definition of success is changing.

- How you define success determines how you define failure.

- Success in Christ is not about the outcome but about faithfulness.

LET'S GET TACTICAL

In the first part of this book, I wanted to help you set a mindset for success. In this next section, we will really focus on specific, tactical things you can do in your Family Business to flourish. Although big business is significantly different than small or family businesses, there are basic business and operating principles that apply across the board. I'm not talking about marketing, finance, product design, or technology; I'm talking about Human Resources. Many organizations consider Human Resources a catch-all or "throwaway" function. Top business leaders are transitioned into leadership roles in Human Resources without any experience in the space. It's often considered a developmental area giving them another function to add to their resume.

When you think of Human Resources, you may think of the person who manages payroll, answers your health insurance questions, and provide the sexual harassment training each year. In reality, Human Resources covers a wide range of critical business areas that can make or break an organization. Without the foundation of solid hiring, development, change management, and performance management practices, the good work that happens across the organization cannot flourish. Human Resources is the worker bee that makes all other functions work. It is often under the radar and unappreciated, but when the wheels start spinning off, all eyes turn to the row of cubicles shoved in the corner. When organizations pay business consultants hundreds of thousands of dollars to analyze their organization, inevitably they come back to talent management practices. Organizations are forced to take a deep look at their culture, hiring practices, development programs, and performance programs. Ultimately, organizations have to take a step back and get those things right before the "money-making" components can move forward. When organizations think they can overlook this quiet function, they often find themselves spinning their wheels. It is so foundational to success that regardless of your industry, business, or family make-up, these principles will help you find success and some of that sanity you put somewhere safe years ago, then forget where you put it.

JOB DESIGN

Myth 10: I am Super Mom. I can (and should) do it all.

Truth 10: Yes you are, but you can't (and shouldn't) do it all.

Since women started returning to work in the 1980s, women have gotten the raw end of the deal. Not only are we going back to work and helping support our families, but we are also responsible for carrying the weight at home. Now I'm not suggesting that this is across the board. There are certainly supportive husbands out there who are carrying the home life as well, and things are certainly starting to shift with more and more men recognizing their role as a partner in, and contributing member of, the family. That said, there is no doubt that a discrepancy in workload still exists. As much as men do in our households, many of us carry a heavy load beyond the cooking, cleaning, and raising the children. When someone stops by unexpectedly while the house is a mess, how often do they comment, "Looks like Kyle hasn't had time to clean today"? Or when the Christmas cards didn't go out, how often do you hear, "I guess Ray was too busy to get cards out this year"? Or how about those end-of-year teacher gifts? How often have you heard a man lament about finding the right gifts for the teachers? Not too often. There is still a bent in our society, and in our own hearts, to carry this weight for our families. I was flipping through an article and within the "suggested" articles I saw a title that read, "Celebrities who raise their own kids without nannies." I felt myself saying, "Good for them" with an attitude of "it's about time". After a minute, I was disgusted at my own reaction.

First of all, what about the celebrity dads who do or don't use nannies? Why are the moms called out? Because she is the one responsible for managing her career *and* the children? "Sure darlin'. You can have a career if you really want to. That's so cute. But you know, you still have to keep those kids clean and fed and keep that husband of yours satisfied." What century is this? I have never even lived in this type of society, yet these deep-rooted tendencies still make their way into my thoughts, words, and behaviors. Secondly, why should she be expected to do it all without help? Technically, I have a nanny. She happens to be my mother-in-law, but I certainly couldn't do it without her. She watches my boys all day, cooks dinner several nights a week, cleans the house while I'm gone, and often helps get the boys in bed. Don't hate. Like many of us, in addition to being mothers, many of the women they called out in this article also wore two or more additional hats. They were actresses, owners of a small business, directors, and wives to equally busy husbands. Yes, raising those babies is the most important, but having help is part of that. Having a career is part of that. Finding fulfillment and meaning outside of the home is part of that. By calling out this extreme behavior as the ideal suggests that somehow, it isn't okay to need help. In reality, all styles are okay and are to be lifted up.

This idea of *doing it all* and *doing it with a smile* has left us with expectations far beyond what is reasonable or even necessary. This is where setting reasonable expectations comes in. This tendency has also made its way into the business world. Perhaps you have seen a job description recently or heard the lamenting of a tired employee trying to get some relief from an expanded workload. "But that's not in my job description". Upon closer examination, you (or they) note the small print at the bottom. "All other duties as assigned." This simply means that *everything* is your job. Partly due to litigation risk and partly due to the need to assign work as they see fit, it has become best practice to add that line to the bottom of a job description.

Aside from the small print, there is a great deal of effort that goes into getting a job description whittled down to the most critical aspects of the role. This is important for hiring but also for providing clarity and direction for employees in the role. When employees aren't sure what they should *really* be doing, it is difficult for them to prioritize and focus on the most critical. This is where it gets serious. As a mom, a wife, an employee, an entrepreneur, and all of the other hats you wear, it is important to understand what the most important things are for *you* to be doing. Not the person in the next cubicle or your friend down the street. What were *you* specifically and uniquely hired (or created) to do? These are the things you should be focusing on. Although we ultimately end up doing a lot of "other duties as assigned", it is important to remember what our most important responsibilities are.

These responsibilities are called key responsibilities (of the job). These may also be called "essential functions". In business, the most critical functions of the role are identified to ensure only the required physical abilities and education/experience qualifications are assigned to the job. We also used to call this the "elevator pitch". If someone stepped into an elevator with you and asked what you do, you have only a handful of sentences to describe what you do before the elevator dings. What are the most important or critical things you would tell them? Would you tell them about your kids or your business? What are the things you wouldn't mention? I certainly wouldn't mention that I take the trash to the curb every Tuesday. Although this may fall under "all other duties as assigned", it certainly doesn't describe one of my essential functions.

It is really important to understand *your* job description. Hear me out. If you were building out your own job description, what tasks or responsibilities would you put on it? In organizations, we often start by listing all of the tasks that comprise the role. As employees think about their roles, they often forget all of the additional activities they do that aren't specifically part of their job yet take up a significant amount of time. As moms, these often include things like being the Public Relations representative for our families, ensuring our children are well educated, purchasing household goods, back to school clothes, and presents, packing for vacations, etc. Be sure to list it all out, even if it's just a task list. Once you have what you believe to be a complete list of your tasks or activities, you can group them into similar clusters. This will make it easier to see the big buckets of similar or related tasks. In the job descriptions I write, this might look something like, "Serve as the financial advisor for the family including paying bills, managing the money, and providing regular updates (let your husband know if he can buy those golf clubs or not….kidding)". I might also add, "Ensure the family has healthy meals every day including grocery shopping, meal planning, and preparing healthy meals". We may also include "Keeping the house clean and organized including keeping up with the laundry, regular tidying, weekly deep cleaning, maintaining a safe and healthy environment, and making all of the beds every day".

Unfortunately, many of us also serve as the spiritual guide for our family, which may sound something like, "Serve as spiritual leader for the family including ensuring my family gets involved in church, teaching my kids how to have a relationship with God, praying at meals, teaching them to be good people, and instilling values". During focus groups with my subject matter experts, we would spend a great deal of time grouping these activities into the top three to five buckets of activities. This information would then be used to value the job, which means determining how much the job is "worth" based on the skills required, decision making, and autonomy. Unfortunately, we will not be conducting any analysis to determine how much this job should be paid. Plenty of folks have run these numbers though, and the consensus is that no one can actually afford to pay a mom.

Okay, so you have your list grouped nicely where possible. Now, take a deep breath. If you feel overwhelmed, you should be. This is too much. I don't care how "short" your list is. You are likely taking on too much. So, let's start cutting some of this out. Unfortunately, it's not always possible to just cut out entire buckets of activities. If so then great! Cut out the entire grouping. Otherwise, you may find yourself following the steps below for individual tasks within a bucket. Consider the groupings nice ways of keeping related tasks close to each other, but don't worry if they get busted up. First of all, identify the things that you enjoy doing and are uniquely positioned to do. When I say uniquely positioned, I am referring to those tasks and activities that you have specific knowledge, skills, abilities, personality characteristics, and experiences that provide you with special capability to accomplish. In an organizational setting, we would say that these are the activities that we are *definitely* hiring someone to do in *this* specific role. There are other important things, but we want someone who *enjoys* these things *and* is really *good* at them. If you were applying for the job, what are the things you would be looking for in the job description? For me, I love to play with and nurture my children. Although someone else could probably do it, they couldn't do it as well as me, but I would also really miss it. That is my special gift, and I love it. I also enjoy the business that I am running. It is a primary part of my description. No one else could do it as well as I can, and I love it.

The extremes tend to be the easiest for me, so I would like you to tackle the bottom of the list next. Identify those tasks that you are neither good at nor enjoy doing. These could be things that anyone could do, and it wouldn't make a difference. For me, these are all things dealing with the house: cleaning, making beds, doing laundry, etc. I do not need to scrub a toilet to feel that I have contributed to my family today. I'm not necessarily *bad* at it, but I'm not particularly *good* at it. I'm slow and inefficient. I don't like it and don't care to get better. Some people *love* to clean. It makes them feel successful and productive. If you are a better person when you personally clean (not when the house is clean but when *you* clean it), then do not scratch this off your list. Eventually you may find that this practice no longer serves you and is taking up valuable time you could be spending elsewhere, but for now, keep it. Take all of these tasks that you don't enjoy and aren't good at and move them to the bottom of the list.

When I was judging flute competitions, we would have twenty to fifty flutes trying out throughout the day. We were behind a curtain and had no name, picture, or sound bite to associate with each player. We simply had a number and our notes. The top and bottom 5% were easy. We could quickly identify them and typically all agree. It was the mess of flutes in the middle that took 95% of our time to sort out. Tiny differences between them were so minuscule. We would spend hours debating a single rating because that rating could ultimately be the difference between making it or not. For you, that tiny differentiation could be the difference between maintaining your sanity and losing your marbles. "But it's just one tiny thing," you may think. "I can do that in fifteen minutes. It's easier than delegating. I'll just do it." Those *tiny, insignificant* activities are the ones that eat up your time, energy, and sanity. It's those little, fifteen-minute tasks that rob us of time on our business, time with our families, and time for ourselves. It is in the mess of tasks in the middle that you must be diligent to carefully evaluate the importance of each one and its relevance to your goals. Take another deep breath, and let's get into it.

Physically put plenty of spaces between the top and bottom ends of the list. You should have a clear differentiation between those things you love and are uniquely equipped to do and those things that you aren't good at, don't like, don't care about, and in which the act of doing them has no meaningful impact on your life. All of the stuff in the middle are things that you may be good at but anyone can do them, you feel that only you can do them (I say it like this because there are a surprisingly few things that truly *only* you can do. I know. It's hard to believe. It was a dry horse pill for me to swallow too.), and you aren't particularly good at. Rather than asking you to rank these, I just want you to move the tasks, one at a time, to either the top of the list or the bottom. Are these things that you truly do need to do or is it something you can find a way to let go of? Go through each of the clusters first. If there aren't entire groups you can move down, go through the tasks within the grouping and pull them out. The groups simply help you organize your tasks to see them more clearly.

As you go through your list, you will likely find the scenario where you want to hold onto something that doesn't particularly serve your goals. For me, this was finances and meals. I really enjoyed looking at my finances. I loved seeing how much money we had, moving money around, paying bills, and managing all aspects of spending. There was comfort in knowing where we stood, but more importantly, I felt a great sense of control. I wasn't sure if I could let this clump of responsibilities go. As I moved down the list, I found that meal planning, shopping, and cooking proved to be particularly challenging for me. I didn't care to cook, though I really wanted to get better. After years of watching *The Food Network*, I hadn't picked up a single tip that improved my ability to satisfy my family's desire to eat out. No one raved about my meals, and I found myself more and more upset when someone "already ate" before sitting down for dinner. I wasn't particularly bad, but there was nothing special about it. I also enjoyed spending hours scouring recipes, dreaming about four-course meals I would prepare, creating in-depth shopping lists, and running from store to store to find the right ingredients. Where cooking was a control issue for me, planning turned out to be a distraction mechanism. Rather than focusing on my goals or my family, I used meal planning as a way to *think* I was moving the needle. In reality, it was keeping me from progress.

I just want to pause for a moment and talk about why this step is so important. We intuitively know that we don't have an infinite amount of time and energy, but somehow, I think we truly believe that if we just *try harder* or work *faster*, we really can do it all and that doing it all is the ultimate definition of success. Somehow by saying we *can't* or *won't* do something, we are letting someone down (i.e., family, society, parents, in-laws, extended family, ourselves). It's like we have something to prove, and being busy and tired has become the norm. We wear them like a badge of honor and compare our "busyness" to one another.

A friend of mine once told me, "Cheryl, you are doing a lot of good things. But for all the good things you're doing, the great things are getting lost." I was indeed busy, but the *great* things I was put here to accomplish were getting buried by the *good* things I was busying myself with. As accomplished as I felt, I was actually getting nowhere. It was like I was spending my life teaching people to stuff envelopes so they could teach people to stuff envelopes so they could teach people to stuff envelopes. There was a lot of teaching getting done, but no one actually stuffed any envelopes. More importantly, why were we even stuffing envelopes?

Through this process, I just want you to remember that by saying "yes" to one thing, you are ultimately saying "no" to another. Make sure the things you are agreeing to do are more important and worthy of your resources than the things you are agreeing *not* to do. In business, new projects are often evaluated through a rigorous cost/benefit analysis as well as alignment with overall business objectives. I'll talk about this second part in a moment, but I want to touch on this cost/benefit analysis briefly. Although this can be one of the most painful parts of any project, it is a critical one. Businesses often understand their finite resources better than we do. You can't just propose a project with a hunch and get the green light. Well, sometimes it works that way, but it rarely turns out well. It really does pay to do your due diligence here. With finite or limited resources, organizations can only accept so many new projects. Each project has to have a very clear business case and show a clear return on investment.

As women, moms, business owners, we often take on every new project someone asks us to do. We get asked to chair the fundraiser committee, teach first-grade choir, serve as treasurer, bake cookies, volunteer on Thursdays, and the list goes on. All of these things very well may be important and significant, but that doesn't mean they are especially important to *us* or move the needle in *our* lives. As you go through each item or activity, consider whether this task/project/ activity is important to you or whether it was assigned to you by someone else. If it doesn't move the needle in *your* life or for *your* family, then consider moving it on down the list. With that, let's get back to that list.

I started with meals. I just stopped planning, stopped shopping, and stopped cooking. Fortunately, my husband and mother-in-law picked up the slack. As it turned out, I didn't really miss it. Rather than giving me anxiety and causing frustration, when someone asked, "What's for dinner?" I was able to say, "I don't know." I didn't feel like a failure for not knowing, I didn't feel like I was letting my family down, I certainly didn't take it personally when they didn't eat, and I didn't feel guilty for not meeting this part of my "obligation as a mom". Now, I didn't stop forever. Eventually, I picked some of it back up, but taking a break like that helped me to see the impact it had on my life and helped me better determine if it was something I wanted to add back in. Raising kids is a family affair. My husband can cook too. My mother-in-law lives with us. She certainly can cook. In fact, when I let go, I learned that she actually missed it. By allowing her to cook, she felt more at home than she had since moving in. Who knew that by trying to be *super mom*, I was actually interfering with her desire to contribute? I also think it's important for kids (especially boys) to see their dads helping out around the house. Whenever I'm tempted to *do it all*, I think about their future wives looking at me. Are they going to say, "Thank you", or "Come on!"? I am certainly grateful that my mother-in-law taught my husband to take ownership of his own life.

Have you made it through your list yet? If you haven't, go ahead and take a moment to go through it. Don't just read past this section and think you'll come back to it. I've done that countless times. Do you know how many times I actually went back and did the activity? None. I promise. You will not regret stopping here and doing this assignment. I'll wait....

Original List:	Divided List:
Part-time job	Teach Bible study
Clean the house	Church orchestra
Shop	Participate in co-op
Cook meals	Homeschool children
Plan menu	Plan family gatherings
Pay bills	Caretaker for parents
Manage finances	Write content
Take kids to practice	
Provide snacks for games	
Run bake sale at church	Part-time job
Buy all gifts	Clean the house
Plan family gatherings	Shop
Decorate for holidays	Cook meals
Caretaker for parents	Plan menu
Write content	Pay bills
Manage website	Manage finances
Write Christmas cards	Take kids to practice
Teach Bible study	Provide snacks for games
Church orchestra	Run bake sale at church
Do family taxes	Buy all gifts
Participate in co-op	Decorate for holidays
Plan vacation	Manage website
Homeschool children	Write Christmas cards
Attend moms' meeting	Do family taxes
Wash Cars	Plan vacation
	Attend moms' meeting
	Wash Cars

Okay. So now you have a clear line between two lists, and those lists should not be equal in length. In fact, the top list should be considerably shorter than the bottom. The top list should *only* be those things that you are good at and uniquely equipped to do. Chances are, you still have too many responsibilities in this section. I encourage you to take one more pass through this part of the list and ask the question, "Does this task or responsibility move the needle of my life in the direction of my goals?" If the answer is no, I would like you to consider moving the item down to the bottom half of the list. With this lens, I ultimately moved my "manage finances" down to the bottom of my list. Although I really enjoyed it and thought I was equipped, but it didn't serve my goals. Rather than being something that moved the needle in my life, I discovered that it was a control mechanism and a distraction. Because I enjoyed it and it was important, I thought that meant I needed to do it. It was hard to move it down, but moving it down does not mean that it is gone. We will address those in a moment. Right now, just take another look at your list with this lens in mind. If after taking a deep look into each one your list is still too long, don't worry about it. This is a living document. There is nothing that says you can't move things around. In fact, you probably will over time. As you practice these techniques, it will get easier to let go. I promise.

So let's take a look at the long bottom section. As I said, we aren't just going to dump these tasks and run. Chances are, many of these tasks still need to get done, but you don't necessarily have to do them. These items will be categorized into two groups: delegate and eliminate. If the task is something that truly does need to get done, identify it as "delegate". Either write a "D" next to it or write the word at the end of the sentence. If you want to color-code it with a highlighter, go right ahead. Let your creative side have some fun. It might be hard to think that someone else can do this as well as you, but the reality is, not everything needs to be done as well as you can do it. I got really hung up on folding my clothes like Marie Kondo after the big boom of the KonMari Method. I would fold them, then roll them, then place them delicately in my drawer. I folded my underwear and socks just right. When my mother-in-law moved in and started doing laundry, I used to feel the fire in my chest when I would open my drawer and see my shirts rolled widthwise instead of lengthwise, and my socks stretched into a ball.

Did my mother-in-law fold them as fabulously as I did? No. Could I easily find my shirts and socks when I needed them? Yes. Did it save me hours a week and tons of frustration doing laundry? Absolutely. In the end, the negative energy my socks were releasing into my drawers from being stretched around each other wasn't enough to take it on myself. Even if it was, I could probably have educated her on my overly sensitive socks, and I'm sure she would have gladly folded them the way I'd asked. In the end, it turns out I couldn't feel their pain and didn't care.

Many of these *delegate* items will be intended for other adults, but many can be delegated to other family members including children. Absolutely find ways to involve your spouse or other family members when passing around responsibilities. As every family member enjoys the benefit of a nice home, they should also expect to carry their weight in the household. At dinner or during a special family meeting, talk to your family about the responsibilities and the need to *share the load*. Your family may have their own task lists to discuss as well. This would be a really great process to go through with older kids. It would be eye-opening for them to see their lists compared to yours. They probably have a very limited idea of what it takes to run a home. Consider this an opportunity for them to gain valuable life skills that they will thank you for one day. Well, their future partners will anyway.

Not all tasks can or should be delegated to family members. Perhaps your spouse also works a demanding job and the housework just doesn't move the needle for either one of you. In these cases, you may find that paying someone to do the task is the best use of your resources (i.e., time, energy, money). Unfortunately, there are probably many of these, and you can't always afford to hire them all out. In my direct-sell days, our leadership would say, "Hire a housekeeper. You can't afford *not* to." Same with an assistant to do those things you don't want to do or aren't uniquely equipped to do. The reality is, sometimes we aren't in a position to do that. I get it. Hiring help can get expensive and we are often putting every free dollar back into our business just to keep it afloat. Go ahead and mark these items to delegate. You may still have to do them for a while, but the ultimate goal is to get to a point where you don't have to anymore. As you do have some extra cash or can rededicate the income you do have, you can begin to prioritize these items and start clearing them off of your plate.

As I discuss family members, particularly spouses sharing the load, I recognize that not all of the women (or men) reading this book have a partner or supportive partner. Many of you are single parents or have partners who live in an alternate universe where they are not supportive for one reason or another. You may be looking at this list and wonder if it is possible for you to delegate any of these activities. My aunt once told me that as a single, working mother, she didn't always have the time or money to do everything that needed to be done. She would often trade for childcare and help around the house. As a writer and artist, she would trade art and articles for childcare. Similarly, my parents traded printed t-shirts for lawn service. Perhaps you can partner with another entrepreneur. Take turns watching each other's children so you can have time to work or have a much-needed break. If you offer a product or service, perhaps you can trade with local childcare facilities or for other goods/services that you need. This is a great option even for those who do have supportive partners, but it may be particularly valuable for those who don't.

As you are identifying the items to delegate, be sure to also identify the person or type of person who will pick up the tasks. If it is your spouse or child, write their name. Go ahead and assign responsibility. When you have your "family meeting", these names may change, but it will certainly help to see how the tasks are falling out. If you are especially organized, group the tasks by each person so you can see how each list progresses. If your task is being delegated to an outside agency, put the name or type of person down if you know it. If not, you may need to do additional research to find the right group or person. Go ahead and note that so you don't leave it blank.

So now you have a list of activities you are going to do yourself, those items you are going to delegate and to whom. Now let's talk about those tasks that can be eliminated. These are tasks that really don't need to be done at all and can easily go away. This may also include those activities that you are involved in that take time away from the more important areas of your life. If possible, clear off any of these commitments if you can. Write the word "Eliminate" or the letter "E" next to these tasks. Many of us were raised to finish what we start, so this can be particularly challenging. You may need to finish out the year or quarter, but make sure to note that you will not recommit when your duty is up. Do not allow yourself to be caught off guard when you get asked to continue. Be ready! If you have not yet started your commitment and find yourself losing sleep over it, I encourage you to be honest with the person who asked you to take on the commitment and step down. It is much better for them to know early on when they still have time to find someone else as opposed to having you half committed and exhausted. I recently had to do this with two separate commitments. It was incredibly hard, but I felt instantly better the moment it was cleared from my plate. A few moments of courage and humility will save you an incredible amount of time and stress.

Another task I was able to eliminate was my self-identified role of being the family historian. I made it my personal responsibility to make memories and retain memories for my children. One way I did this was through journaling. I started this while I was pregnant with each and regularly wrote them a journal entry about their life at that point. I also had teachers and family write notes at certain points. This task within that responsibility made it to the keep section. I enjoyed it and was uniquely equipped to do it. Scrapbooking, on the other hand, made its way down to the *eliminate* list. At one point I was passionate about scrapbooks. I meticulously cut out scraps of paper and taped them into beautiful patterns to make tiny pictures behind a sheet of film. I sorted and printed pictures for hours. During one of our moves, I had an entire bookshelf of scrapbooks. It occurred to me that I no longer enjoyed this practice, and I was doing it for my kids who may not even want scrapbooks when they're thirty. It certainly didn't move my life needle. Ultimately, I crossed "scrapbooking" off of my job description. At first, it stung. I felt like I was letting my boys down. After a while, I felt the relief that I didn't have that pressure on me any longer. The journal would serve that purpose for them. My mom also reminds me that instead of bookshelves full of scrapbooks, I have family and vacation pictures throughout the house for us to enjoy now! Isn't that just like a mom to remind you of how awesome you really are doing? Thanks, Mom! I love you!

I also found tasks I was doing that fell on the "important" list of others. I was doing things that others deemed valuable. I had never considered whether or not I should be doing them. This is where others' expectations of us sometimes find their way to our list. We don't even stop to consider whether or not they should be there, and suddenly we're left living someone else's life. I have a friend who went back to work after she had kids because that's what women in her family had always done. Stay at home moms were frowned upon (by other women!), and she didn't even stop to consider not going back to work. By going through this process, she discovered that she was working for the sole purpose of fulfilling someone else's expectations of her. Her family could make it without her income, and she wasn't particularly fulfilled by her j-o-b. Ultimately, she found it at the bottom of her list and was forced to really evaluate why she was doing it. Another friend discovered that "decorating for holidays" was at the bottom of her list. She always felt obligated to do it even though she didn't like it and wasn't particularly good at it. After discussing it with her family, she discovered that she could eliminate 80% of the holiday decorating she was doing. A few interior decorations were more than enough for everyone. Talk about a relief! I personally love decorating, so I don't get this at all. But that's irrelevant…

As you look at your list, you may be a little disappointed by how few "eliminate" items you see. It took me a moment to realize that I actually had another list of things I was doing that didn't even make my task list. Things like watching television, surfing social media, reading food blogs, writing out my task list 100 times, and spending hours planning my life down to the month we would have another child. My brain knew they weren't tasks, but if I took an honest look at my day, I spent a good deal of my time doing these things. Typically, we won't list the obvious things we should eliminate because we know they really aren't part of our *job description*. I encourage you, though, to take a moment to go through this list as well and consider eliminating many of these activities as well.

Once you have your list of tasks to eliminate, keep them at the bottom of your list. Don't delete them. If you delete them, when the thought pops in your head in a day, week, or month, you may forget that you have already considered the task and deemed it unnecessary. You may scramble to your list and try to figure out how to insert it back into your day. By seeing it on your "eliminate" list, you can put your mind at ease that you have already done your due diligence to evaluate and eliminate that activity. If, for some reason, you need to move an eliminated item back up the list, go ahead. This is your list, not mine. No one is going to think poorly of you. Just be sure to go through this process again to ensure it is necessary.

Example Eliminate & Delegate List:

D - Clean the house - Maid

D - Shop – Spouse / Auto

D - Cook meals - Rotate

D - Plan menu - Spouse

D - Pay bills - Spouse / Auto

D - Manage finances - Spouse

D - Take kids to practice - Friend

D - Game snacks - Spouse

D – Wash cars – Service

D - Buy all gifts - Spouse

D - Manage website – Web Guy

D - Family taxes - Accountant

D - Plan vacation – Travel Agent

E - Attend moms' meeting

E - Part-time job

E - Christmas cards

E - Run bake sale at church

E - Decorate for holidays

One final piece I would like to touch on is automation. You may not be able to scratch off entire tasks, but there are likely still ways you can make the tasks that you are doing faster and easier with less brainpower. This process is called automation. I was working with an external consultant on a project. We were doing some pretty mundane tasks of sorting and organizing rows and rows of data. For me, it was easy work where I could just daydream or sit in front of the television and copy/paste from one spreadsheet into another. I didn't mind it, and it helped me feel useful. The consultant, on the other hand, was paid out by the average time it took to complete a project. The faster he could get it done, the sooner he could go soak in the hotel hot tub while still earning the rest of his project fee. I was up most of the night copying and pasting. Although it wasn't hard, I was pretty tired of doing it after eight hours straight. He showed up to the office the next day refreshed and full of energy. I asked how long it took him to complete his portion, and he said it took about two hours. In disbelief, I pushed him, to which he finally admitted creating a macro. Being technologically ignorant, I had no idea what it was. Basically, he created a little program to do exactly what I was doing by hand. The basic computer software doesn't necessarily do all the fancy stuff we needed done, but it is customizable in this way.

He explained how he taught himself how to create macros, and sometimes it takes a little while to set up. It took him some time to learn, but in the end, it saves him a ton of time. For one project, it wasn't worth it to me to even learn how to do this specific macro. The project was over, and I wasn't going to take the time to learn it for so little gain. I'm sure you can see where this is going. Two weeks later, the consultant was back with another batch of data that needed to be compiled. One all-nighter wasn't terrible, but looking down the barrel at another one was too much for me to take. I asked him to show me how to set up the macro, and I too reaped the rewards of a little extra time on the front end.

Maybe creating macros for spreadsheets isn't where your automation value lies, but I guarantee there are areas in your home and business life where you can implement a few practices to make certain tasks run more smoothly. One example is to set the slow cooker timer so that you can put all of the food in first thing and have it kick on at noon. For a long time, I fought this feature because I thought it was weird to have raw food sitting in my slow cooker for four hours before it started. Then I would run out of time to come home or have to stop what I was doing to get everything set up. After scrambling a few too many evenings, I decided to give it a shot. This tiny program has been a life-changer for my meal planning and dinner routines.

I had a co-worker who *always* had a clean email inbox. How was this even possible? It turned out that she set up a folder for people or groups who emailed her frequently. The incoming emails would go directly into that folder, and a small number in the corner of the folder would alert her to new emails. No dings, pings, or flashes. When *she* was ready, she would scan the folders for new emails and check them when her brain was ready to address that type of issue or need. Although it felt like too much work to learn a new system, it was an ingenious way to reduce the clutter and compartmentalize her work allowing for her most productive workday.

I know several folks who use email templates for responding to frequent requests. By setting them up as various templates (given your server capabilities) or even putting the entire email in the signature section, you can quickly select the appropriate template and hit send. This is particularly valuable for those requests in which you provide a great deal of information such as blog links, websites, or tools. This can also be done through Word documents saved on your computer, but it may be faster within the email system itself.

If you have things you do all the time, take the time to create an automated system for it. Send email automatically to different folders, create processes to make it easier, schedule when you will clean so your kids know and do it with you, set up Amazon ordering so you have your refills delivered. Take the time to set up processes that will save you time on the back end. It is also important to automate yourself when it comes to your schedule. Set timers to know when to move from one project to the next or for important appointments. That way you aren't constantly looking at the clock or anticipating the end of your work time. When I have to look at the clock or check my phone for the time, I inevitably get distracted with an alert or notification outside of what I was initially checking it for. Additionally, any time your brain has to stop and change tasks, even if just to check the time, it's easy to lose the flow that you had before. That short amount of distraction, multiplied throughout the day, can result in a lot of lost productivity.

I want to touch on distraction briefly. When we check our phones, email, or social media, we run into things to react to. When we are just about to make a breakthrough or settle into a rhythm, we distract ourselves. If we have a difficult thought or are facing something hard, we often distract ourselves. It's easier to check our phones or respond to an email than face the reality of our situation or push through a block. When we do this, we are training ourselves to let go right when something big is about to happen. Just when you are about to complete an important thought, just when you are about to face a tough emotion, just when you are about to learn something about yourself, you turn away. Researchers found that test subjects picked up elevated levels of arousal several seconds before students switched to something else. It's like your brain is *trying* to keep you from expanding and growing. The more we do this, the less able we will be to focus in the future. We create the *habit* of distraction, which means it becomes an activity of the fast-processing part of the brain – the subconscious. We don't even think about it anymore. We just feel it and avoid it. What's more, a study by Hewlett Packard and the University of London found when we divert our attention to incoming calls and messages, it actually dings our IQ by 10%; that's twice the effect of smoking marijuana.[12] I don't know about you, but as a tired mom and entrepreneur, I need all the IQ points I can get!

By turning off your notifications, putting your phone on "do not disturb", and limiting outside distractions, we can teach our brains to focus longer and more intensely. In this way, being focused can become a habit too.

For a long time, organizations focused on hiring candidates who had specific experiences and technical skills required to perform the job. As organizations are developing, they are discovering that it's actually the soft skills, not the hard or technical skills that differentiate between successful and unsuccessful employees. Soft skills are those skills and abilities that enable us to engage with other people, connect data and information, and understand the world around us. Some examples of soft skills include interpersonal communication, decision making, critical thinking, problem-solving, and conflict resolution. Many even consider attitude to be a key soft skill and one that Industrial Psychologists like me are working tirelessly to accurately measure and assess. Technical skills, on the other hand, refer to those related to the completion of a specific job or task. Soft skills are developed over time and require a wider range of experiences to fully develop. Many of these are also personality characteristics that are the result of upbringing. It is significantly more challenging to develop soft skills. The development of soft skills requires actual practice and a great deal of self-development. Technical skills, on the other hand, can more easily be achieved through training and rehearsal. Rather than focusing on technical skills, organizations see greater results when they focus on hiring for soft skills.

As entrepreneurs, we understand the value of these soft skills. Many of us have little or no training in running a business or the particular area of our focus. It is the soft skills that have enabled us to achieve a certain level of success. Even so, entrepreneurs often suffer from imposter syndrome. Imposter syndrome is the fear of being discovered as a fraud. Although you believe you are capable, you doubt that you are as qualified as you should be or as qualified as others think you are. Perhaps you even feel unworthy of your success. Both genders suffer from imposter syndrome, but women tend to be more susceptible to it and feel the effects more intensely.10 Imposter syndrome is common, but it does not have to control you. Some suggestions for combating imposter syndrome, particularly for women include owning your success. When someone gives you a compliment, don't shrug it off. Receive it. Simply say, "Thank you" and don't attempt to explain away your success. Another tip offered by Forbes Magazine is to take your seat at the table. Rather than sitting at the back of the room and waiting to be called on, sit on the front row and use your voice. Body language is a huge giveaway of low self-confidence and can make you look insecure, even if you don't know you are doing it. Stand tall and physically take up more space. As women, we tend to make ourselves as small as possible by folding our legs and turning sideways. Meanwhile, men take up twice the amount of space their bodies should. They command the room while women try hard to appear invisible.[13] Most importantly, know that you deserve to be where you are; you deserve to be at the table. You would not be where you are if you weren't fully capable and equipped. Believing in yourself is the greatest combatant against imposter syndrome.

I encourage you to sit down and make a list of your soft skills. What experiences, attitudes, abilities, and personality characteristics do you bring to the table? Perhaps you are steadfast through trials and doubt or maybe you are incredibly agile and adaptable. Perhaps you have incredible interpersonal communication skills and can command a room by simply walking in. Don't explain them away. Confidently identify your strengths and write them down. When you are faced with doubt or fear, pull out this list and remind yourself of the incredible person you are. Remind yourself of your abilities that reach far beyond technical skills.

Take a moment to do that now.

I also encourage you to make a list of those technical skills that you possess in the field of your choice. It's likely that there are others that have more experience or knowledge in one area or another, but that is irrelevant to the knowledge *you* bring to the table. Without comparing yourself to others, identify the unique knowledge, experience, or training that makes you qualified to operate in your field. I am positive that if you are honest with yourself, you will identify more knowledge than you initially thought you had.

Go ahead and make that list now.

Finally, I encourage you to make a list of the successes you have had throughout your life, however minor you may feel they are. Use this list to remind yourself how far you have come and what you are capable of. When things are particularly challenging, it is easy to forget our wins. Searching the deepest corners of our minds, we often pull out every failure we have had since we started learning to feed ourselves. As our list grows, our confidence declines. We need to continually fill our pipe with positivity. Every single day, I encourage you to pause at the end of the evening and write down all of your successes for the day. Remind yourself how much you accomplished. Remind yourself that you are still moving forward in the direction of your dreams.

Some days will slap you right in the face and completely knock you off your feet. On those days, and every day, instead of reviewing that negative, yucky list, I encourage you to pull out your growing list of successes and meditate on the vast wins you have experienced in your business, home life, or j-o-b. We don't have time to be held down by false, negative beliefs about ourselves. Our mission is too great; our purpose is too important. Choose to focus on the positive.

Summary:

- Defining your *job description* is critical for understanding what your true role is as a mom, wife, and entrepreneur. Eliminate those tasks that you don't enjoy, aren't uniquely equipped to accomplish, and that don't move the needle in your life.

- You do *not* need to do it all. It is likely that others can effectively perform many of the tasks that you currently take on, and there are plenty of others that can go away completely.

- Imposter syndrome impacts female entrepreneurs. Combat its effects by owning your success, taking your seat at the table, displaying more powerful body language, and believing in yourself.

DR. CHERYL LEJEWELL JACKSON

CHANGE METHODOLOGY

Myth 11: Making a change really isn't a big deal.

Truth 11: There's more to it than that.

There are almost as many change methodologies as there are organizations implementing change. Okay. That is a ridiculous exaggeration, but the point is, there are many. This is because change management is such a critical piece of making a program or initiative stick. For centuries, the philosophy was that if an organization needed to make a change, they simply implemented the change and expected everyone to get in line and do it. That isn't the way it works anymore. Employees are considered an integral part of the change process. There are many pieces of the change management process. It gets complicated and heavy. Organizations spend months and years planning for a change. Although I do believe in the power of preparation, one significant difference between small business and big business is, well, the difference is big.

Small businesses have fewer layers and fewer stakeholders. The small business is nimbler, and communicating to the entire organization can involve walking into the living room and saying, "Hey everybody. Gather round for a minute." Rather than taking weeks to schedule a meeting to get approval to schedule another meeting in a few weeks, all approvals can be a matter of looking over a coffee cup and asking, "Would you mind taking a look at this quickly?" It just doesn't take as long to go through each of the steps.

Although it can be a bit easier and faster to begin the change process, truly implementing and making change in your family or small business takes time and focused energy. There is no short cut to change. Within our families and small businesses, we rarely think of change as being a well thought out process. We have an idea, discuss it a bit, and tell everyone what we are doing. When our children, spouse, or employees struggle, we take the "do it because I said so" approach. As one of the primary decision-makers or even the *only* decision-maker, we have the expectation that our decision will be respected and adhered to without question. In reality, people are people whether they are wearing their *family* or *employee* hat, and they need to be treated as stakeholders. Although companies frequently skip this process, significant change is rarely as successful as it could be when stakeholders aren't treated as such and aren't taken through a specifically designed process for gaining their understanding and acceptance. As I mentioned, there are many different change approaches, and they can be very complex. This section is intended to provide you with a foundation or start to understanding change. There are books and programs focused on implementing change that would be more valuable for a more in-depth understanding if that's what you are looking for. This section is intended to give you a nice overview and simply start the discussion.

There are two distinct types of behavior change that organizations often seek when investing resources into a change process. I say "behavior change" because ultimately, organizations are not interested in doing something unless it results in actual, measurable changes in behavior intended to advance the organization in some way. Even in the case of changing values, making work more meaningful, or changing the company branding, organizations are expecting some sort of behavior change that will ultimately lead to more profitability. Many organizations have begun implementing a volunteer program whereas employees get time off to volunteer or serve as a group. Rest assured that most organizations are not going to invest in a program like that unless they intend to receive some sort of payback in terms of improved productivity or reduced turnover. These efforts are often the result of hours of focus groups and research showing that these branding colors or volunteer programs make the organization more attractive to employees or customers. Companies don't just invest in something for the sake of it. Okay, occasionally a CEO (chief operating officer) will come in and change the color scheme because they don't like purple, but you can bet she hired some researchers to back up her desire so she can convince the board to buy-in. What I am talking about applies to most organizations across the board, but the public organizations have an extra layer of protection against making decisions just for the sake of change. This is the Board of Directors. They oversee significant decisions to ensure they are in the best interest of the company (i.e., will make them more money).

Although small, family businesses aren't always thinking strictly about behavior when making a change, it is a good practice to get into. Sure, you may decide to change your logo because it just doesn't *sing* to you, but as your business grows, it is important to focus your resources on those things that are going to produce the greatest outcomes. Changing the font in your logo may make you happier, but it could also serve as a distraction, helping you avoid doing what is really going to propel your business forward. If you are trying to make a change with your family, business, or yourself, get into the practice of defining the behavior change you are interested in, not just the outcome you hope to produce.

I will provide an example related to implementing a healthier lifestyle because that is one most of us are all too familiar with. Throughout my life, I have tried just about every diet in existence. If it even hinted weight loss, I was in. Although I understood the components of the diet that equated to behavior change, I was ultimately focused on the outcome. How much weight do people lose on this diet? How many inches do they lose and how fast? There was a component of behavior change, but it wasn't my primary focus. I knew what I had to do to get the results I wanted, according to the diet plan. So, I set off to eat *only* those things or not these things, always watching the clock tick and the scale hardly budge. In reality, there is so much more to only eating or avoiding certain foods at mealtimes. I needed to define the behaviors that must change in order for me to be successful. At a party, what will I physically do to avoid food? When someone asks me to lunch, what will I physically do to make the right choices? By outlining the actual behavior change that needs to happen, you can more easily begin to see the bigger picture for the change.

Creating a new habit, you have to write down current behaviors and those to change. When I get bored, I eat. I will instead go for a walk, take a bath, or read. At a party, I eat more than I should. Instead, I will walk away from the food and visit with someone in another room. When I get home late, I don't want to cook and end up eating out. Instead, I will cook meals on Sunday to have them ready to go all week. There aren't only behaviors you must *start* doing but likely even more behaviors you first need to *stop* doing. You can't just *add* healthy food to the mix.

In one program, this process of identifying stop and start behaviors ahead of time is called "creating an *Emergency Action Plan*" or EAP. Know what you are going to do before you are put in a situation of temptation. Establish your "escape route", memorize your mantras, and practice your lines. Know what you are going to say when someone asks why you aren't enjoying the cake. You must be prepared to stop the negative or old behaviors and replace them with positive, new behaviors. Making a change is difficult until it becomes a habit. I have heard people say, "Living by habit is so sterile and boring. We have free will for a reason." I would challenge this by saying, "You are already operating by habit. It's just a matter of whether they are good habits or bad habits." I walked into the bathroom one morning and noticed my three-year-old had missed the big hole in the toilet quite severely. I initially reached for the toilet paper but quickly realized that it would not be substantial enough. Instead, I grabbed the hand towel off of the ring and wiped the toilet seat down. Instead of tossing it on the floor, I draped it on the edge of the counter so I could grab it when I headed out. I proceeded to wash my face, as I do every morning.

Right before I was going to open the drawer and grab a fresh towel to dry my face, my son walked in and started talking to me. I turned to face him. With water dripping everywhere, I grabbed the towel and, well, it was nasty. If I can wipe my face with a urine-soaked towel out of sheer habit, it tells us that habit has a *very* strong hold on our lives. Have you ever gotten to thinking in the shower and lost track of where you were? I couldn't remember if I had washed my body yet. I smelled the loofa and examined it for moisture content. I rubbed my armpits to see if I could detect any lingering deodorant. I couldn't tell, so I washed my body again. Then, wouldn't you know it? I couldn't remember if I had conditioned my hair. Did I usually condition *before* or *after* the body wash? I honestly couldn't remember. Most of our behaviors are pure habit. That is what allows us to spend our energy on the things that really matter. It's when we can turn productivity and positive behaviors into habits that we will start to see exponential improvement in our lives.

Back to the two distinct types of behavior change. The first one is transactional or compliance-based. These are changes that need to be made for compliance purposes as rules change or when a better, faster process is identified. There is no emotional reason to do it one way over the other, so the faster, safer, or easier way is better. A financial, safety, legal, or logistical reason for the change is usually enough to get the needed buy-in and begin the process toward change. When pushback occurs, the classic response, "Because I said so," is often used and doesn't interfere too much with the ultimate implementation of the change. One program refers to this change process as "the hammer". Because these changes are often based on changes in laws or safety requirements, using a "hammer" to enforce the change is an effective approach. The change simply has to be made. If you don't follow the rules, you will lose pay, be fired, not get dessert, not get to attend a party, or lose your bonus. Implementation is based on punishment for not doing it the new way, and eventually, the change becomes a normal operating procedure. Although change is often hard initially, these changes don't typically require a change of belief or mindset. Therefore, this change process is considered simply transactional.

If a new software program is implemented, use the new program. If we are no longer creating reports on the 2nd and 4th Fridays but rather the 1st, 3rd, and 5th, then run the reports on a different day. There are many transactional changes that we implement regularly. Right now, my father-in-law is trying to get my boys to take their shoes off in the same place (their room) when they walk through the door. As I heard him saying it one day, I looked at my shoes piled in a corner by the garage door. If he cares that much, I guess I should take my shoes off in my room too. As much as I wanted to make it an argument based on principle (this is my house; I can put my shoes wherever I want), I quickly realized that this was simply a behavior change that I could easily implement, creating a new habit that I soon wouldn't even have to think about. It was hard to start making the change, but it wasn't really a big deal. I didn't have to meditate or change my values to meet that request. If a change can take place without too much initial buy-in, then the change is transactional and requires a bit less effort on your part as the change management lead. That doesn't mean you don't still need to follow some of the same steps, but you may not need to stay on those steps as long.

The second type of change is transformational or commitment-based change. These changes are those that require helping stakeholders understand the *why* behind the effort. The employee must have a thorough understanding of the benefit. They need to know what's in it for them and understand the *why* behind the change. Without a careful process of preparation, these change processes rarely work for long. Team members must be fully bought into these changes to be successful. It is often the case that employers attempt to use the "hammer" or punishment to enforce these types of changes. Unfortunately, this can have the opposite result as people rebel or dig their heels deeper into the current way of doing things. Perhaps you are familiar with the idea of parents *forbidding* their teenage daughter to date the town rebel. The classic result is that this only serves to push the daughter further into the arms of her bad boy. There is a delicate balance between pushing too hard and not enough on these types of changes. It takes time for these changes to become a habit because there are more moving parts.

Several times, I have tried to get my family, particularly my husband, to eat better. I would explain that we didn't have the money for him to eat out every day, I would remind him how unhealthy it was, and I would attempt to guilt him into being healthier so he could live to see our boys grow up. I would pack his lunch with fruit and carrots, set out a healthy breakfast, and even send him with an afternoon snack and special treat, just to keep him from going off the rails. For dinner, I would prepare his favorite meals, remove carbs in the evening, and I wouldn't buy junk food to have around. He would agree that eating healthier was important and he would try. Off he would go with his lunch bag, and I would feel pretty proud of myself. The first day he would come home with empty sacks and eat my dinner. Soon he would eat my lunch but stop off on the way home because he was too hungry or wasn't excited about dinner. Eventually, he would plop a full lunch bag on the counter and admit to stopping off at lunch *and* on the way home. Before bed, he'd polish off the ice cream he picked up somewhere in between. Most of us can relate to this. Not only for trying to get our families to eat healthier but ourselves too!

This type of change is so hard because it is transformational. It requires a deep belief in why we are making the change and a true acceptance of the need to change. Even then, it's still hard. Behavior, good or bad, becomes habit, and that habit becomes our lives. When we have engaged in certain behaviors for a long time, it is always a little challenging to change, regardless of how badly we want it. When a change requires significant effort and focus, we need the buy-in even more. It takes constant vigilance to not slip into those old patterns. Have you ever headed off on an errand and remembered that the road is closed on your typical route? This transactional change requires no real commitment, and your habit still had you take the old route. Because you have no options, you turn around and go the other way. It isn't emotional, just a bit annoying. Now have you ever been on a diet and found yourself pulling into a fast food joint when you felt a hunger pang or a bit of thirst? I certainly have. If deep down, you know you want that burger, it's harder to pull yourself out of that line. You have to be deeply committed. It also helps to have some accountability factors at play to give you that extra push. This is where writing your food down and sharing it with someone else has a way of helping enforce change. The hammer can't be the only enforcing device, but it can help give that push toward behavior change. In these cases, it's referred to as "accountability" rather than the "hammer". Even though it does help enforce, it is more of an emotional push than a compliance-based one. Telling your friend that you had an ice cream cone isn't going to cost you your job, but you will have an ache admitting that you let yourself down. Sometimes true "hammers" also work here. There is an app where you earn money for sticking with your health goals. If you achieve the goal, you receive some money, but not achieving your goals costs you even more. These tools attempt to tackle this most difficult transactional change from a number of angles. Truthfully, that is often what it takes.

As you attempt to make a change with your family and/or business, it is important to take some time to understand if this is truly a transactional or transformational change. Unfortunately, we tend to make things transformational on the basis of principle. "I'm not going to take off my shoes here because I don't want to do what you said." It feels like a constant struggle for even the simplest activities. In this case, it may be necessary to get at the heart of the matter, which is a change in attitude and obedience. It is not about taking the shoes off here but rather treating each other with respect. By tackling the larger, more difficult aspect of the behavior, the rest becomes a bit easier. I have had to address this with myself recently. My in-laws moved in with us a while back. It had always been something that I looked forward to, though I did not account for how hard it would be. For many months (too many), everything that I had to change about my routine, my home, and my life felt like personal attacks. I didn't want to change, and I held it against them. I felt that I had lost my home and control of my life. I couldn't do the things I used to do and had to develop new routines and behaviors. It felt like everything was changing and I had no control over anything. My home, my safe haven, was no longer that place.

Because I was holding onto this deep sense of loss, every change was magnified. Rather than it being about the change, it was adding to my loss of control and freedom. It wasn't about moving laundry off of the table, it was about being told what to do in my own home. Everything was tied to the bigger issue. Instead of addressing the real issue, I let the smaller events eat at me. I felt completely justified in my feelings, and I may have been. Regardless of whether I was justified or not, tying innocent events with deeper issues wasn't healthy for me and wasn't fair to everyone else. It took a while, but I began to heal that part of me that felt invisible. I had created a habit of being angry before anyone even said anything. In anticipation of having to speak before my first cup of coffee, I was angry before I even heard movement in the kitchen. Even though I hadn't addressed the deeper issue yet, I had to separate it from the individual request or change in front of me. I had to stop connecting everything and blowing up over a simple question or change in my routine. Once I started seeing some of these changes as transactional, I was better able to treat them as such and release my aggression and hostility about it. It wasn't and still isn't easy, but it has made life more enjoyable for everyone, especially me.

Once you have identified the behaviors you are interested in changing and understand the type of change you are after, it is important to define your stakeholders. These are the people who will be impacted by the change either because they are the ones changing or they are impacted by the result of the change. How will they have to act or think differently? At times, we implement changes not fully understanding the downstream effect it has on others. I help out at a food pantry, and one of the other coordinators and I crafted an entire plan for how to serve more clients each week. We took the plan to the pantry coordinator, and she blew it up. By walking us through her activities, we were able to see the downstream effects of our simple change. Although the line would move faster, it added hours to the setup and tear down process. Had we moved forward with the change without including her, it would have created a lot more work for her, and probably some pretty sour feelings toward us.

Identifying the various stakeholders is a time-consuming process that many organizations overlook. "Well, they have to do it anyway," is the response many leaders give when we discuss the need for this step. Sure. Ultimately, they probably do have to make the change anyway, but by clearly outlining each person or role and the impact on them, you can better prepare for making the change, but you may also find areas where the impact is too great or unnecessary. Maybe there is a better way to serve more clients without adding this much extra work to one group. If nothing else, understanding the impact will aid in the communication process. Talk about the impact with the stakeholder. Let them know that you are aware of the extra work and appreciate their added effort. Let them know that you have explored other options but there just aren't any. This type of conversation goes a *long* way to helping stakeholders accept the change. They still may not like it, but it does make them feel better about it, and they will be more likely to follow through.

When it comes to change, one thing impacts success more than any other, and that is sponsorship. If my father-in-law is trying to get my kids to take off their shoes in their rooms, but my husband and I don't care where the shoes go, it is going to be really tough for him to get traction. If they see us leaving our shoes wherever we want, they think it's okay for them to do too. If they drop their shoes on the floor right in front of me, and I don't reinforce the change, they don't see the change as important. Leaders promoting the change are called sponsors. Individuals within the organization are called champions. Champions are also critical for reinforcing change because they tend to be the people that the rest of the organization looks up to. As important as champions are, without leadership sponsorship, the change is likely to fail. Ultimately, if the leaders don't care, there will be no benefit to making the change. It won't affect my paycheck, and I won't get fired for it, so why should I do it? As the parent, you are your child's top tier of leadership. Although other adults such as grandparents, teachers, and other family members do play a significant role, if you aren't reinforcing something, it is likely not going to stick. Your role, as a sponsor for other change efforts, is critical. Your role as sponsors for each other is even more critical. You must support each other and face change as a united front.

Many organizations implement change and move on. Some programs refer to this as *installation* rather than *implementation*. Unless there are really good punishments or rewards in place, the change will drift away without proper follow-up. With any change initiative, there is an initial phase of resistance. This occurs because change is always a little challenging, and it takes time to settle in. Think of this as the opposite of the honeymoon phase. This effect is magnified if there has been a history of change without follow-up. Stakeholders may wonder if this is going to stick or not. It's not worth making the effort to change if it won't matter anyway. Folks certainly aren't going to make an emotional commitment to something that isn't going to stick around long. This is an important one as small business owners. If you tend to bounce around a lot, it is hard for your family to get behind any individual effort. I tend to get excited about a lot of things. I have done a number of direct selling ventures, I join any committee that makes a request, and I like to volunteer wherever I feel pulled, and I also like to have multiple jobs going on at a time. I call it "diversifying my portfolio". I have also gardened, gone "waste-free", recycled, done Fly Lady, taken up several diet and exercise regimes, blogged, and the list goes on. My schedule is always bulging, and my husband ends up picking up a lot of the slack around the house. Although he is always supportive of my dreams, it is hard for him to get excited about the extra hours he will be putting in to support that dream. He does it, but when I go on and on about my exciting venture, it takes him a while to get on board. He needs to see that it's going to stick before he lets himself get too excited. I often decide that it's not for me and move on to something else that I am equally charged about.

If you are a dreamer, know that not everyone is wired the same way that you are. Not everyone sees the value in doing something just for the sake of doing it, trying something new, or saying, "I did it". Those around us often get caught up in our wake as we flutter around like dancing chickens. I have to be doing 800 things at a time or I feel stifled inside. I just can't imagine going to work, coming home, hanging out, reading, and going to bed. As nice as it sounds, I know I won't feel complete. My husband, on the other hand, can't understand my need to have seventeen plates spinning at one time. We are just wired differently. I can get excited about something in two seconds flat. For him, it takes a lot of thought and time. He has to see it work before he gets on board. He also has to know that it won't interfere too much with what he wants, which is time with me. (Awwww.) It's easy to let the spinning plates take over and forget that time with family is also a spinning plate that can't be dropped. Sometimes we think we can set that one down for a while and still expect them to be 100% supportive of our dreams. That really is asking a lot of mere mortals.

That was a pretty lengthy tangent to say that sometimes you receive resistance to change because you have established an environment where the past has suggested that this change won't stick. Sometimes people just need to see that the effort matters. This is where follow-up comes into play. Follow-up allows you to measure resistance, let others know that the change remains important, and reinforce the behavior change you are after. We will talk later about performance management, which is a process of reviewing performance expectations. When organizations implement change, they include those anticipated behavior change in the performance review process. This allows the behaviors to remain front and center in the mind of employees and managers. It goes along with the saying, "*inspect what you expect*". Regular touch bases allow you to discuss any behaviors that need to be adjusted before they get too engrained. Part of the performance review process is also to receive feedback on your style as a leader, the work, and the decisions you are making. This includes the change itself. Many managers don't receive feedback because they don't ask. By opening the conversation up and asking for their thoughts, often people will tell you. If you don't ask your family how they feel about something, they may not come out and say it. Instead, it comes out in the form of frustration or resistance. The simple act of giving them an opportunity to share their feelings often goes a long way to making people feel better about a change.

I will dig into the performance evaluation review later, but I do want to make the connection that it is a critical component to implementing a change. There must be a reinforcement strategy in place. As new behaviors are encouraged, those behaviors should be reinforced. They become part of the values, culture, and expectations, and they are modeled by those in leadership positions. This is imperative for the success of any change process whether transactional or transformational. Research shows that 70% of all major changes in organizations fail. This is in large part due to a lack of a plan including failure to define a clear rationale for change, ignoring the existing culture, weak follow-through by sponsors, not investing resources in the change effort, lack of agent skills, and haphazard communication. As important as a good change plan is, major changes in an organization can also fail due to failure of feedback, declaring success too early, and neglecting to reinforce the change. This sounds pretty complex, but by simply engaging in a bit of pre-work and walking through these steps of the change process you can dramatically improve your chances of successfully implementing change within your family or small business.

Summary:

- When implementing change, identify and define the specific behaviors you want to see.

- Determine whether the change is transformational or transactional as the type of change drives the way you go about implementing it.

- Define a reinforcement strategy and follow-up approach to support the proper implementation of the change initiative within your family or small business.

DR. CHERYL LEJEWELL JACKSON

SETTING EXPECTATIONS

Myth 12: I have to be awesome at everything.

Truth 12: No. No, you don't. It's okay to be okay. It's also okay to be not
okay. It's also okay to be awesome. It's okay to get better.

I once heard Rachel Hollis (whom I adore!) say, "If you're going to do
something, why wouldn't you want to do it the best you can?" Initially, my
instinct was to nod my head in agreement and shout, "Yes!" After settling
down from my excitement, I started to feel really defeated. As I got into the
car that evening, I thought, "Man. My car is really dirty. I should clean it
up." As I cooked dinner that night, I thought, "Oh man. This isn't my best.
I should take a class." As I gave my kids a bath and my mind drifted, I
thought, "Focus Cheryl. You should be a more engaged mom." As I fell
asleep without waiting for my husband to come in, I thought, "You sure are
a lousy wife." How quickly it progressed from excitement through
negativity and down to complete and utter defeat. In spirit, I absolutely
agree. If you are going to have kids, start a business, homeschool, take a
job, get married, absolutely give it your all and try to be your best. When it
comes to other things that "just need to get done", perhaps those "other
duties as assigned" we talked about, it's okay to not be awesome. As
women, I believe we often take a good message and blow it way out of

proportion. I recently saw a quote by *Peaceful Mind Peaceful Life* that read, "Doing your best does not mean pushing yourself to the point of mental breakdown." To this, I shout, "Yes!"

At one point, I wanted to be a better cook. I actually thought I enjoyed it, and it's such an important part of my family's life, I definitely wanted to apply the "be your best" philosophy to it. As I reviewed recipes, tried new techniques, and beat myself up, I realized that I was letting other, arguably more important things, fall by the wayside. I was allowing my "other duties" to become my key responsibilities. I was giving the extra activities more of my time than they deserved. When it comes to some things, like folding laundry, being your best isn't necessarily critical. When we think it is, we sure do put a lot of pressure on ourselves. It is okay to just be yourself, like the *good* self, and not the *awesome* self that you would give to the higher priority activities. We have a finite amount of energy in a day. Don't waste your time trying to blow everything out of the water. Focus on what's really important.

We talked a bit about this during the job design chapter previously. When I asked you to go through your tasks and identify those that you are both good at and uniquely equipped to do, we were essentially focusing on those activities that are your strengths. Recent research has brought attention to the idea that focusing on improving your strengths instead of improving your weaknesses is actually more productive. When you work on improving the areas where you are weak, research suggests that you can only bring them up so far.[14] You likely won't ever be great at these tasks. Rather, the end goal in developing these areas is to be *not bad.* Of course, this is a generalization and there are *many* areas you could likely develop into strengths. Generally speaking, though, areas of weakness develop more slowly. While you are spending time developing your weaknesses, you are

130

under-utilizing your strengths and not advancing your primary goals because you are spending that finite energy trying to move the needle from *bad* to *not bad*. When it comes to living your best life and stepping into who you were made to be, being "not bad" isn't exactly the goal I had in mind.

By focusing on your strengths, you can actually move the needle from "good" to "great" and make a more significant impact on your work, life, and family. Organizations regularly evaluate their strengths and pursue those products, programs, and initiatives that support them while letting go of those that didn't really take off. There is actually a book called, *From Good to Great* that discusses how these organizations made a come-back by focusing on these very things. Somehow, I don't think a book entitled *From Bad to Not Bad* would do as well.

So, do we just ignore our weaknesses and pretend they don't exist? Not necessarily. Although we encourage our managers to focus primarily on strengths, there are critical weaknesses that certainly should be improved in order to meet at least minimum thresholds. In some areas, without meeting certain minimum levels of performance, it could be difficult to be successful. In these cases, it can certainly be beneficial and necessary to strive to make improvements. I struggled with closing the sale at my direct-selling appointments. It was a weakness for me but a critical part of the sales process. Because this was such a critical part of making my business successful, I had to spend a significant amount of energy making improvements in this area. I slowly began to move the needle, but it required a great deal of focus. Even then, I achieved the greatest gains when I focused on my strengths within that activity such as active listening and filling the need. When it comes to other areas, it may not be worth the focused effort. Spending hours working on my cooking at the cost of improving my writing skills, for example, would not be worth it. I am never going to be a world-class, blue ribbon-winning chef. At best, I may not burn two out of three batches of cookies instead of all of them. For you, it may be something completely different. The spirit of this section, though, lies in those moments when you are making decisions about how to spend your finite energy. We all have areas of weakness. That does not mean there is something wrong with you; it simply means you have strength in another area. Where focusing on your weaknesses can tear you down, focusing on your strengths can lift you up and is much more powerful.

I encourage you at this point to take the time to think through your strengths. Perhaps look back through your key responsibilities and tasks. What do you do really well? You may also find these at the bottom of your task list in those activities that just don't align with your greater mission and purpose. I'm not asking you to do all of these things; just have a good understanding of what they are. We don't highlight our strengths quite enough IMHO (in my humble). We often rattle off our weaknesses at the drop of a hat but don't give ourselves enough credit for the incredible talent that we do have. It might even be easier to ask a close friend or family member what your strengths are. I often have a hard time hearing it because I think, "Oh if they only knew". This is often that imposter syndrome sneaking in and stealing our confidence. Having a strength does not mean we are perfect in that space. It simply means we possess some special skills, abilities, or talents there. Other people often see these areas more clearly than we do because they don't feel all of the insecurities or hear the self-talk we experience. If/when you ask for this input, don't question it or try to deflect. It may be uncomfortable to hear, but it is important. Take a moment to reflect on your abilities, express gratitude, and just sit with the reality that you are already pretty freakin' awesome!

Now, this part might come a little easier, or it might be a little hurtful to think about. Without judgment, write down some of your areas of weakness. Sometimes we call these *development areas* or *opportunities* to soften the blow, but we're all big girls here. Call them what you'd like. Identify those areas where you could definitely use some improvement. Many of these areas can be found in the bottom part of your task list. These are things that you aren't particularly good at and might even be *bad* at. You struggle to do them and might not enjoy the process. When it comes to improvement, the process of improving or outcome itself doesn't even appeal to you. These are those areas where added time and energy spent working to improve doesn't move the needle in your life very much. I want you to take a moment to reflect on these areas or activities. Express thanks for the opportunity to learn more about you, and release yourself from thoughts of inferiority around these areas. Let go of the pressure you feel to improve and any doubt you have about yourself because of these areas. Take a moment to sit with the reality that there are areas where you may be less capable and know that these areas do not define you. They are a small part of a bigger picture. If God had wanted you to be strong in these areas, He would have made you that way. He made you the person you are, perfectly equipped to fulfill the plans He made for your life.

I encourage you to take a moment and look through the task list you created earlier. Reflect for a moment on what makes you particularly good at a specific task. Is it your technical ability or perhaps your soft skills such as focus or resilience that we talked about earlier? Think about what contributes to your key tasks being strengths for you. Really dig into why certain activities come with ease or are particularly enjoyable. Break the task down into individual components to have a better understanding of where exactly your strengths are. This will give you a deeper understanding of your development areas as well.

In learning and development organizations, we often focus on developing soft skills rather than technical skills. Yes, there are technical components, but the sweet spot is much more fundamental. Take project management, for example. In the many classes I took, we spent a surprisingly small amount of time learning the specific steps and talking about how to fill out the spreadsheet. Instead, we focused on the *why* behind the activities. We focused on developing focus, attention to detail, and problem-solving. In my sales days, we focused on the fundamentals of closing the deal, but the real advances were made when we learned the art of listening, identifying a need, and filling that need. This goes far beyond the technical aspects of asking a list of questions and filling out a sales slip. Similarly, we can almost all relate to the challenges of learning to drive and/or teaching someone to drive. If it was about pedals, switches, and gears, it would be a lot easier. Unfortunately, there is so much more to driving. Deductive reasoning, planning ahead, and awareness of surroundings are not technical skills but rather critical soft skills that are instrumental to success. By focusing on developing these underlying capabilities, you can advance farther in your development than you would by focusing only on the technical aspects, which are also less likely to transfer between tasks.

It's no surprise that most people, not just moms, want to be great at everything. At one point, our performance review process had a nearly infinite scale. Managers could choose any value between one and ten and take it to two decimal points. This meant that managers would spend hours and stress about one 100th of a point difference in someone's rating. As in 3.93 or 3.94. They would spend energy perfectly aligning their team so that the point-difference between employee ratings was reflective of actual, justifiable differences between the employees. Instead of focusing on each employee, it was about balancing them across employees. Although I applaud their effort and diligence, this process was completely unnecessary for effective performance discussions. So, one year we changed the scale to a three-point scale: Needs Improvement, Meets Expectations, and Exceeds Expectations. No half points, no almost; nothing in between. As you can imagine, some people loved it and a lot of people hated it. Some saw the change as freedom to make a decision and move on. Others felt a complete loss of control and viewed the change as the removal of their ability to manage their team as they saw fit.

I think we often get that way too. We want to know exactly how we are performing in a specific area. We want to know if we are close to the next level and how close. We want to know how we compare to others in similar roles. We want to know exactly how much we have improved since the last time we were evaluated. When in reality, there are only three categories: got the job done, above and beyond, or needs to change. Even when it gets the job done, we often criticize ourselves for not doing it better. Just like performance review scales, our self-evaluations are based on the established expectation. It is important to determine what level of performance is actually required for each activity. It may be a surprise to some of you, but exceeding expectations isn't always required or better. When my mother-in-law first started doing my laundry (I know. I'm grateful every time I say it.), she not only hung my clothes but also color-coded them and sorted by occasion. It was nice, and I appreciated it, but it was unnecessary. In this case, going above and beyond, or "exceeding expectations", didn't really add anything. When I would do my own laundry, I struggled to maintain her categorization and ultimately went back to what fit my needs.

Employees often struggle with a rating of "meets expectations" because it feels a lot like "average". Inevitably, people want to know how to move to "exceeds". 1.) That isn't always necessary and 2.) "Meets expectations" means that you are doing exactly what you were asked to do. Once the expectations move up, the criteria for meeting and exceeding expectations move up too. It's not static; it's based on the established expectations or criteria for success. Theoretically, those criteria are updated every year based on employee capability, previous performance, and new needs. "So, the better I perform this year, the better I have to perform next year to get the same rating?" Well, yeah. That is often the case. Your performance becomes the new norm, and the expectation increases. This is why clearly established behavioral expectations are critical. Left to our own devices, expectations can continue to increase unnecessarily. In the introduction for this book, I mentioned the phenomenon where a new factory employee may get dinged for working too hard and pushing the daily quota for others. Without established expectations, leadership could easily bump up the expectations daily based on the standards for the day before. Even though it may be *possible* to produce faster, it may not be *necessary*. Likely, an organization is going to push people as hard as they can because it all comes down to money, but we know that there are so many other, more important things such as engagement, health, and life itself.

During a performance review or evaluation, employees are rated on goals associated with those key responsibilities identified in their job descriptions. Therefore, exceeding expectations truly could be a reasonable goal. In our case, we often evaluate ourselves on things that are completely irrelevant to our overall success or to moving the needle in our lives. In the corporate world, we would never rate an employee on how well they took out the trash or how clean their desk was. They may get "talked to", but those would be irrelevant components of their performance review because they are not critical to the job they were uniquely hired to do (unless they are a custodian or desk model). The only time it would come into play is if it interfered with the performance of their job. If they are seeing clients at their desk, for example, and those clients are turned off by the mess, then that would be interference. In my case, having a cluttered desk directly interferes with my ability to think clearly and write effectively. Therefore, I usually pack up and move to Panera Bread since I'm not so good at keeping organized and tidy. It works for me now, but I do recognize this is a "development area" in which I do need to spend a bit of energy moving from "terrible" to "not bad". I may also find value and enjoyment in avoiding the technical skills of actually cleaning and focus instead on the soft skill of organization. Somehow, I might have missed the spirit of this section.

As a psychologist, I try to take the subjectivity out of everything: assessments, hiring, firing, and performance evaluation. One criterion for being objective is that someone else can get the same result you do. This is a critical component of research called "replication" and means that your results weren't a fluke or unique to your specific situation. Have you ever had an issue with your vehicle? You take it to the mechanic and he says, "Ma'am. We don't see the problem." You swear up and down that the car makes this sound at idle, "Clunk, clunk, clunk," and this sound when you hit the gas, "Vreeek, squeal, vreeek, squeal," and shakes like this when you get up to speed, "Shake-a, shake-a, shake". As accurate as your description and sound effects may be, if the mechanic can't replicate it, he can't fix it. It may do it for you, but if it doesn't do it for anyone else, or when someone else is around, then it's considered a fluke. Only when a mechanical issue is replicated can it be corrected, and only when results are replicated can they be generalized to other, similar situations. To do this, we put different measures and criteria in place. Everything is clearly defined, and no stone is left unturned. In business, this is critical because we want to hire the best person for the job, and we don't want that dependent on who is doing the interviewing or administering the assessment. Everyone deserves a fair shot based on their skills and abilities. To the untrained eye, objectivity often feels "overkill" or unnecessary. It also feels cold and sterile. I am here to tell you that it doesn't have to be. This is one of those practices that can really add some sanity back to your life. When it comes to our self-evaluations, we are not very objective at all. We take the worst part of our day and call ourselves "failures" or base our success on our inability to cook a steak to medium-rare. Believe me, to a steak-lover this is an important ability, but it is not the basis for your success.

For the purposes of this section, I want you to focus on your role as a mom, wife, or entrepreneur. Just pick one for now. If you are like me and tend to be harder on yourself as a mom, then I encourage you to pick this area. If you feel pretty darn confident in your "mom-ing" skills (and I pray we all get to that point), then pick another area where you struggle. Now think about those most critical, key responsibilities you defined in the job design section. What are your primary duties, responsibilities, and activities? For each one, define what success looks like. Get down to the nitty-gritty here. Does it matter to you if your child's hair is combed or does it matter to others? Do your children need to be fully dressed all day or can they run around in their jammies, diaper, shirt? Do they need to know their ABCs before they start kindergarten or are you okay if they learn it there? Yes, let research have input into your decisions, but it can't be solely based on that. Children may be *more* well-adjusted if they can read by three years old, but if that is your only driving force, you will drive yourself crazy trying to hit that marker. Give yourself some grace and set expectations that you can live with. Always know that statistics are just that. With all else being equal, children who (*fill in the blank*) tend to be better (*fill in the blank*). You can usually change the story or statistic for your situation by adding or changing something else. Don't be so focused on doing the *right* thing based on research or the opinion of others. Trust yourself and your bigger picture. I love research and statistics, but there is always more to the story. How do you define success in this space? What risks are you willing to take? What can you live with or without? Don't get crazy here and write down your dream situation. Only write down those behaviors or results that would "meet expectations" for you. You can always bump up the criteria, but for now, set it and stick to it!

Now, do this exercise for all of the important areas in your life. What does success look like to you as a mom, wife, entrepreneur, friend, daughter, community member, Christian, etc? You don't have to get down to the task level for each of these, but I encourage you to take a moment to really understand your definition of success. When you begin to feel the urge to compare yourself to the supermom next door, go back to your criteria for success and evaluate yourself against that. Physically pull this list out and look back at your definition of success. Did you meet *that* criteria today? Sure, there may be other areas you would like to improve and perhaps didn't do these perfectly, but did you consistently meet expectations? If so, congrats Momma. You are doing it! If not, put yourself on a little *Performance Improvement Plan* (PIP) and get to work. It doesn't mean you aren't doing a great job, it just means that there are areas in need of improvement. A PIP is simply a commitment to yourself that you will work on one to two areas. Not *all* areas but one or two specific ones. Define how you will work on them and the outcome for which you are striving. Make sure that anyone else looking at this would rate you the same way, based on your criteria, not theirs. Don't be harder on yourself than your established criteria. Evaluate yourself objectively and confidently know that you are doing a great job!

I actually started doing this exercise for vacations and holidays as well. I tend to set extremely high expectations for myself and my family. I plan excursions, activities, crafts, campfires, reading books, fixing our marital problems, learning to love each other, and speaking a new language into a three-day trip. When someone wants to sleep in, I throw a tantrum and feel like the trip is a failure. I really had to step back and identify just a handful of things that would mean success for me. When I really sat down and evaluated what was most important, time together inevitably floated to the top. The most important memories to make are those where we are together. It didn't even matter what we were doing. Sure, there are always some key things I want to fit in, but that number has dropped dramatically along with their individual significance. By changing the lens by which I evaluated these things, I discovered that it was much more successful than I had ever imagined.

Summary:

- Not every activity requires a rating of "Exceeds Expectations".

- Focus on developing your strengths and soft skills over weakness and technical skills.

- Set clear expectations and criteria for success for yourself. When tempted to compare yourself to others in a specific area, look back at *your* definition of success.

PERFORMANCE MANAGEMENT

Myth 13: Performance Management is micromanaging. I trust my team or family to do what needs to be done.

Truth 13: You must *inspect* what you *expect*.

Most organizations have some form of performance review or performance evaluation process. In large organizations, this is frequently referred to as Performance Management. Although organizations tend to do this better than most individuals and families, it is still one of the most despised processes by leadership and the employees they support. I'm sure you're familiar with this process if you have worked in any formalized capacity. I worked at my parents' screen-printing shop from the moment I could hold a paintbrush and fold a shirt. Each year, I would get a more challenging task. I didn't realize it back then, but my parents were setting expectations, monitoring my work, and giving me more challenging assignments as I developed. It wasn't as formal as it is in larger organizations, but there was a process all the same.

I once managed the performance management process for a large retailer employing at that time over 250,000 employees. I managed the process for temporary, hourly employees in the stores all the way to the

CEO. I can tell you from experience, organizations would get rid of this entire process if they could. They hate it. The fact that they don't get rid of it but instead spend hundreds of thousands of hours translating to millions of dollars a year in time and hard expenses certainly suggests that this process is indeed valuable and worth the investment. Although I don't anticipate you will have any interest in implementing such a formal process complete with associated software, there are components that transfer nicely into the family and small business. These components include setting goals in alignment with overall vision, regular follow-up, and supportive goals focused on activity.

When organizations set long term goals, it is referred to as their vision. In alignment with that vision, they set a series of goals including twenty, ten, five, and one year and even quarterly goals. In public organizations, this process is quite extensive and involves a room full of analysts, journalists, and recording devices. When the CEO makes a projection, things quickly go into motion, and billions of dollars are directly impacted by those goals. Chances are, your goals are not scrutinized by the entire world, but they are no less important. Perhaps you want to have more family time or grow your business this year. It is critical to define that goal and the steps that will be required to make it happen. In organizations, that typically involves rolling goals downhill. Each executive gets a set of goals directed at their specific part of the organization or their contribution. That executive rolls goals down to their teams, etc., until each individual contributor has a set of goals designed for their contribution to the larger business objectives. Some organizations are getting better at this by actually defining pillars or business objectives that each individual goal must be aligned with. This serves the dual purpose of ensuring each individual goal is indeed aligned with the organizational strategy, but it also gives the individual something bigger to align with. Rather than seeing their individual tasks as the task itself, they see it as supporting the business objective. They can clearly see the alignment rather than the "pie in the sky" alignment.

As I mentioned, within organizations, there are strategically developed business objectives. Business leaders get together to discuss these goals, which are often developed over the course of several months or even years prior to implementation. Although I wouldn't anticipate it taking this long within your family or small business, the point here is that these goals do take time and careful consideration to develop. They should be strategically and thoughtfully defined with the long-term vision in mind. This is when your vision or mission comes into play. What is the culture you are trying to establish? What is your long-term vision for your family and/or small business? Where do you see it in five, ten, fifty years? It is critical to have a long-term vision in mind when defining these goals. It might be fun to expand in a different direction, but if it does not align with the overall vision you have, either reconsider your vision or reconsider the move. If you are reconsidering the vision, which happens *way* more in organizations than you would think, then go *all* the way back to that step. Do not move forward with goals until you have a clear vision in mind.

Although we have created a long-term vision, goals need to be less *distant*. In order to move toward those long-term goals, it is necessary to pull that goal backward. Where do you see your business in ten years, five years, next year, and by the end of this year? What is the vision, and what are the steps that need to happen to bring that vision to fruition? Most of the organizations I have worked with use the SMART goal process when defining goals. You have probably heard this before. The *S* represents *Specific*. If I am trying to get healthy this year, my goal would not be to "Get healthy". That is not specific enough to know whether or not I have achieved the goal or not. If my softball coach had defined, "Get better" as a goal, we would not have known if we had achieved that goal, even with the tracking and charting. What does *get better* mean? So don't set a goal to *improve sales, gain more followers, book more gigs*, or *grow as a family*. Really define what success looks like in that goal. Really get objective with this. Someone looking from the outside should be able to say whether or not you hit that goal, even if they know nothing about you. It is critical to take the subjectivity out of this goal because we have a way of normalizing our current reality and being harder on ourselves. For some reason, many of us have a hard time giving ourselves the credit we deserve. By identifying specific goals, this allows us to objectively evaluate whether or not we achieved a given goal. Specific goals from the previous list could read, *increase* sales by 25%, *increase followers to 400, have ten gigs booked for next year, drop 55 pounds*, or even *exercise for thirty minutes four times a week.*

Classically, the *M* in SMART represents *Measurable*. For years I taught goal-setting this way, highlighting the need to be able to measure the results of your goal. Based on the way we evaluate projects and success in almost every other area of business, this didn't raise too many eyebrows. Several years ago, though, I heard a trainer put a little spin on this. He referred to the *M* as *Meaningful*. Instead of driving home the value of measurement, which is effectively represented under the *specific* section, he discussed how important it was for the goal to be something that is *meaningful* to you and will *motivate* you to strive for it. I couldn't believe I didn't think of that! Since then, I have gulped the Kool-Aid and fully preach the importance of setting *meaningful* goals.

The *A* represents *Action-Oriented*. Goals must have steps you can fulfill to complete it. There are few things more frustrating in a job or in your business than to have the outcome completely dependent on something out of your control. If you find that your goals have no real steps that you can take to make it happen, it is not a good goal for you. Sure, many goals have components that are out of your control, but the majority of steps should be things you can control or influence. There are also goals that are ultimately only partially influenced by our actions. *Gain 400 followers*, for example, is ultimately influenced by things outside of our control. If people don't move to their computers to follow your blog, then you will not reach your goal. That said, there are steps you can take to do everything in your power to influence that.

The R represents *Realistic*. I am the top offender when it comes to establishing goals that are about three light-years away. I am an *all-in* kind of girl. I just know that if I put my head down, I could achieve anything. And that's probably true to a certain extent. But when life gets tangled between sick kids, a husband losing his job, in-laws moving in, me getting sick, and priorities shifting, I feel like a failure because *I didn't try hard enough*. Yes, goals are supposed to be stretch. They motivate us to put in just another hour or work for thirty minutes instead of watching another rerun. They inspire us to wake up before the sun and make that last phone call. Unfortunately, they can also be discouraging if they are too high. If you set goals that require you to be on your better-than-best game 400 or even 300 days out of the next 365, that is not attainable. That is insane. Rather than serving to *encourage* you, it may do the opposite. When you realize you are already two weeks behind after three and seven weeks behind after twelve, you start doing the math, and it's just not good. "What's the point? I'm never going to reach my goal anyway." Having goals you can achieve does not mean they should be easy, but it is important to have some wins along the way. Be sure your goals are stretchy, but not unattainable.

The *T* in SMART stands for *Timely* or *Time-bound*. This means that our goals have time-limits to them. When we write a goal, we need to write *by when*. What is the deadline for this goal? As we break that goal into steps, we have timelines next to those. As the saying goes, "A goal without a deadline is just a dream". As an avid dreamer myself, I struggled with putting deadlines on my dreams. I felt that it took away the excitement and adventure. I wanted to dream in far-away galaxies. After a few decades of making little progress, I finally realized that until I reach the stars, I would never make it to the galaxies. Until I sat down and defined my steps, I would be floating in outer space forever, just wandering around like a lost little astronaut. As fun as that was the first thirty years, I didn't want to spend the next thirty just wandering. Even then, it took me another ten years to sit down and apply the knowledge that I have used to help organizations flourish. Why was it so easy to help others but not myself? That is a question I still struggle with, though by focusing on goals, I have a clear path forward.

Once you have defined goals for one year out, take those goals and break them into smaller steps. Where do you need to be at the end of each quarter and at the end of this month, week, and eventually, today? These steps become smaller goals that will help keep you on track. Although you may not be on track with a given day, week, or month, you will still be able to see how you are moving toward your goal. You may be off this month but still on track for the year. By breaking goals down, you have an opportunity to see much more quickly when you are getting off track. Rather than getting to the end of the year and saying, "Man. I missed that goal!" you will see much sooner whether or not what you're doing is going to get you to your goals.

I recently tried to get rid of some of my old notebooks. As I flipped through them, I found notes, journal entries, and a *lot* of goals. Man, I had big dreams! I hate goals, dates, affirmation statements, and even what my reward would be. As I flipped through the various notebooks that spanned more than twenty years of my life, I noticed a sad theme. Almost every set of goals was the exact same. I wanted to get in shape, start my own business as a writer and speaker, and travel. They were even in the same order, most of the time. Occasionally there would be an additional goal in there or the specifics would be spelled out more, but they were the same. My mom later brought me a box from high school. Wouldn't you know that I found the exact same list in a notebook from high school?

I can even remember carefully writing those goals each time. Once I took a personal retreat over New Year's Eve just to reflect on my goals, my dreams, and my future. I prayed about each of my goals and asked God to shine a light on what He wanted me to do with my life. I wrote those goals down and committed myself to not forget. The next page in my notebook was from a client meeting at work on the job descriptions for the Global Security and Aviation organization. I was working out the description for Planners, ironically. And that was the last time I had mentioned my goals until the next dramatic goal-setting session. I had goal *setting* down pat. That was not the problem. The problem was in the *doing*.

So how do we keep our goals fresh and alive? How do we live them every day? That process is performance management. Not the system your organization may have used or the tension-building annual meeting that looms on your calendar like a wild cat ready to pounce. I'm talking about the often overlooked, most important part of the performance management process. That process is the follow-up. Good managers know that they must inspect what they expect. The things they ask about, the things they talk about, those are the things that get done.

One step organizations often miss is regular check-ins. These are weekly or monthly check-ins devoted to specifically discussing goals and providing feedback on performance. Some leaders would argue with specific check-ins saying, "We talk all the time. We don't need this." Others would hold the mandatory quarterly and annual check-ins but blow right through the regular touch bases. Ultimately, they often miss the most important part of performance management, and that is keeping it alive. You can always tell the importance of a project or goal by how often it was checked on. The longer the time between discussions the more the goal falls to the wayside. We would often have complaints from employees saying that they didn't even talk about their goals all year. They would get a "needs improvement" rating, but they thought all year that they were doing fine. The manager would put them on an improvement plan, but the end of the year was the first time they even knew there was trouble. I would always tell managers, "You must *inspect* what you *expect*".

My boys were playing with a box of blocks in the toy room. I told them to put all of the blocks up before we left. At two and three years old, I'm not sure why following up didn't immediately come to mind. I called them to load up, they came running, and we left. After I put them in bed that evening, I glanced into the toy room and noticed the box of blocks was still strewn all over the floor. Not surprisingly, the next day it happened again, and again, and again. I don't know why I expected them to just do it. Well, I know why. I had a habit of telling them to do something and then not following up. I thought about how often I tell them to eat their meat and then let them get down without doing it. I rarely followed-up to make sure they actually did what I told them to. Not only did I not enforce the instruction, but I didn't praise them when they *did* do what I asked. They had no reward or punishment either way. I wasn't showing them that it was important. Why would they do it now? I was training them to ignore me.

Similarly, I had trained myself to ignore my goals and plans. I rarely followed up on myself. When I did, I just got discouraged. Just like our children need to be monitored for following the rules, we need to monitor ourselves. Not all of us are gifted with self-discipline and focus. Even if we are, we may use that energy for keeping our children alive rather than meeting a challenging work goal. Keeping self-promises is the most important thing you can do for your self-esteem and self-discipline. We talked earlier about breaking goals down into months, weeks, days, and even hours if necessary. We do this so that we can keep the goal top-of-mind but also to have multiple check-ins. If we begin to get behind, it's much easier to notice that after a week if we have specific goals to check in on. The key here is to actually check in on it. In each of my journals, I had goals broken down and even plans for working out at 6:00 AM, writing on Saturday afternoons, and traveling here with this bonus check and here at Christmas. I had it all planned out. The problem was, I never looked back at that page in my notebook. I merely wrote the goal again next time I felt "behind".

Within organizations, managers often hold weekly one-on-one meetings. This is an opportunity for the manager and team member to go over their projects and provide updates. Although this isn't directly focused on the specific performance goals, they are typically in alignment with the goals established and allows for the employee to stay relatively on schedule. We worked hard to train managers to actually refer to the goals at least monthly, but often this occurred quarterly, at the half-way mark, or only annually. This is still better than what many of us do, which is set goals, feel down on our birthdays or at the New Year when we see another year come and go, and sternly promise ourselves to not be in the same place next year.

Rather than being a time of encouragement and reflection, it becomes yet another opportunity for us to berate ourselves.

Part of breaking goals down is to have specific landmarks to hit, but it is also to give us little opportunities to be successful. When we achieve those smaller goals, it's a little self-confidence boost. Self-promises are the most important ones to keep because they have such a profound impact on how we feel about ourselves. By setting smaller goals and achieving them, we have many opportunities for repairing the damage that years of negative self-talk has created. Slowly, we can begin to build that self-confidence that comes with honoring self-promises and having real, tangible success.

We talked quite a bit in the previous section about setting goals. Most of these goals are focused on an outcome. Classically, these have been the goals that we set because it's the outcome we really care about. We did, though, talk about the importance of the "how" in the values section. The *how* can be just as important, and even more important, than the actual outcome. So it's not always just about the outcome but how you got there.

When you set goals based on outcomes, there are things that can get in the way of reaching those goals that have nothing or little to do with your performance. Often, we would get to the end of the year and a significant project was cut or never implemented. My manager would look at me looking at her. A goal that was not achieved, for whatever reason, would fall under "needs improvement" for sure. When it comes to situations that are out of the employee's control, that just doesn't fly. Employees must be rated based on their work toward that goal. I often had employees call me with these concerns. I would have to speak with the manager to understand the reasoning for the ratings. If the employee was right, I would explain that they couldn't rate the employee down due to things outside of their control.

It just isn't fair. Yes, it logically makes sense, but we would lose a *lot* of good employees if we took that approach. It would also do significant damage to innovation because employees wouldn't be willing to take risks. Instead, they would learn to only attempt the safe, "sure things". Ultimately, this can destroy creativity and a culture of innovation.

When it comes to setting goals, there is certainly one component that is about the outcome, but an equally important component is about the activity or the steps along the way. My goal one year was to publish my first book. My supportive goal was to work on my book for at least ten hours a week to meet that goal. That included writing in the early stage, editing, creating supporting material, searching for an agent, etc. I also had deadline goals along the way, but the activity goal was consistent throughout. Publishing a book depends on many factors, not all of which are within one's immediate control. The more the goal depends on other people or circumstances, the more important the activity aspect of the goal becomes. Another example is when I was building a direct-sale business. I had personal goals of recruiting so many team members and selling a certain amount of product. Some months I missed those specific goals, but I always met my activity goals. This would be the number of phone calls or the number of bookings each day, week, etc. When your activity goals are set correctly you typically do have a better chance of meeting your outcome goals, but at a minimum, you will be moving the needle in the right direction.

I mentioned earlier in this book that God defines our success by our faithfulness. Remember that His plan is bigger than any one moment or setback. When things don't initially appear to be going in the right direction, I encourage you to remember that as long as you are still faithfully moving forward, you are fulfilling God's expectations for you. Do not be discouraged by the immediate results, or lack of results. When it comes to raising children, being a woman of integrity, or running your small business, the outcome isn't always the focus. Instead, it is the how and the actual work itself. In those moments when things just aren't lining up for me, and I begin to question my purpose and success, I imagine myself at the pearly gates of heaven. I can hear God asking me about my time on earth. With tears in my eyes, I admit that I didn't meet my goals or live up to my full potential. I imagine God coming over and giving me a great big hug and saying, "My sweet baby girl. Didn't you know that it wasn't about the outcome? Every day that you walked the earth, you had a chance to fulfill your purpose. It was about the people you met along the way, the lives you changed every day. It wasn't about reaching a specific destination; it was about the people you touched along the way." I encourage you to not get so focused on the end goal that you lose sight of your true purpose in this life; to reach people for the Kingdom of God. If you gain the world but don't love, you have gained nothing. Keep walking, but walk carefully.

Summary:

- Set goals in alignment with your vision.

- Follow-up on those goals.

- Remember that the true goal is not about the outcome but about the steps you take along the way.

PROJECT MANAGEMENT

Myth 14: I have a plan in my head.

Truth 14: HA! I believe you have a plan in your head. And if you keep it there, that's where your dreams will stay.

In business, project management is a fast-growing career field. For every project, program, or idea, a project manager is assigned to walk it from idea to implementation. If you have ever worked with a company to remodel a bathroom or published a book, someone likely served as the project manager. A plan was drawn up, a budget was established, critical stakeholders were identified, and a timeline was set. I'm not suggesting the plan was always perfectly followed, but in all likelihood, a plan was created.

How often though, have you gone through a similar process in your home and business life? Have you outlined a communication plan for your social media activity? Have you outlined a plan with deadlines and goals? If you are like most moms and entrepreneurs, you have not. We often don't see ourselves as project managers. "I don't need to *manage* it; I just need to *do* it." The reality is, everyone is a project manager. It just so happens that you are often the designer, approver, implementer, and evaluator too. Perhaps you sketched out a plan or idea in your calendar or on the back of an envelope. Maybe you even jotted down some steps in an Excel spreadsheet. Unless you are *very* disciplined, Type A, or OCD, in which case you probably aren't reading this book because you have it all together anyway, then you probably have not even looked back at that sticky note since you wrote it. I would even venture to guess that you probably don't even know where it is. I am speaking from experience here, not judgment. I am so familiar with this that it's hard to even laugh about it. As organized as I want to be, and often was at my j-o-b, when it came to my side hustle or family goals, I just couldn't manage to follow through with the tried and true techniques that I used at work.

Yet, despite my failure to implement this technique, I still managed to be pretty successful. I managed to accomplish goals, keep people in the loop, and follow (kind of) an established budget. What I didn't have was a sense of sanity. I was frantic about missing arbitrary deadlines. I always felt behind; like I hadn't been making any progress at all. When I had a few minutes to work, I didn't know where to begin. I wasn't sure where I left off, I couldn't remember the next steps, and by the time I figured it all out, I heard the faint sound of feet pounding against the bedroom wall, and I knew my youngest was up from his nap, banging his heels against the wall, and ready to p-a-r-t-y. I somehow managed to be fairly successful, but I lacked the focus and organization that I leaned on at work, which cost me a great deal of sanity.

Looking back now, I don't know why it didn't occur to me to implement these practices at home. For some reason, it felt different, sterile, and completely unnecessary. Sure, it was helpful at work, but home is not work. I didn't want to be at work; I wanted to be home. Why would I bring work processes home? But if it worked there, why *wouldn't* I want to give it a try? If you're still with me, let's get into the project management process.

Previously I talked about evaluating your task list and writing your "job description". As I mentioned there, it is critical to carefully evaluate your life activities. These can include projects for your business but also those you are taking on outside of work such as volunteer committees, sports clubs, and even hobbies. If multiple steps are involved, you can (and probably should) create a project plan and evaluate it against specific criteria.

As I mentioned, in organizations, leadership carefully assesses the value-add of each and every significant project. A project manager is assigned, and the rigorous process of justification begins. This process includes defining things like the number of resources it will involve and for how long, total cost, expected return on investment, why you, other projects your organization will *stop* in order to complete this one, primary risk factors, justification for why this project is needed, pain-point it is solving for, anticipated timeline, and the list goes on. It can take a great deal of time to simply get a project proposal developed, submitted, and approved. The proposal development phase for one of my projects took almost nine months. I don't know about you, but I grew a whole person in less time than that.

How many times have you taken nine months to evaluate the value of a project you were considering? Hopefully not that long, because that's ridiculous. The spirit of the process, though, is that careful consideration of the cost and benefits as well as the alignment with our overall objectives is something that we don't carefully consider when taking on new projects within our lives or businesses. Is this the right time to remodel the half bath or replace the front door? Do I have time to join the women's ministry committee at church? Should I lead this Bible study or volunteer at the food pantry? Should I start my three-year-old in soccer or wait until he's five? When it comes to business, should I write a book or focus on my blog? Do we expand by adding a new product or location? Should we rebrand or stick with what we have? Just about every question can be considered a project, even if only for the justification process. Take the time to understand the scope, create a business case, evaluate the cost/benefit, and examine whether or not it aligns with your overall objectives and strategy. With finite resources at your disposal, carefully guard your time with only those things that have a meaningful impact and move the needle of your life.

Once you have determined that a project is indeed worthy of your finite resources, carefully create a project plan. Project plans are more than an outline of steps and dates. If this is as much as you do at first, that's a great start! As you get better at implementing these business practices, you can expand your capabilities in this space and ultimately see greater benefits. We will dig deeper into time management techniques later, but project plans are a great way to build out exactly how you will spend your time when you do sit down to work. When it comes to big or even small projects, there are often many moving parts. Even if you aren't bringing in a project team to help support the project, which in many cases you should (i.e., delegation), a project plan is a great way to establish priorities, keep stakeholders informed, and stay on track.

The first role of the project manager is to establish the project vision. This is often referred to as the "Charter". In this initial phase of the project, the purpose of the project is clearly outlined along with critical elements like timelines, budget, resources, and stakeholders. Sometimes these elements are not clearly defined because critical team members often need to help establish true timelines and budgets, but this step gives a solid overview of the project details. In this process, the audience is defined along with other stakeholders such as decision-makers and those ultimately impacted by the project.

As I was writing my first book, I had a rough project plan, but I failed to fully consider the stakeholders. I thought I was really the only stakeholder. In reality, there are many. My husband and mother-in-law were impacted because they had to pick up more of the responsibilities around the house while I was working. My boys were impacted because I didn't spend as much time with them. Both would be impacted by the success of a book resulting in money, travel requirements, interviews, celebrity status, paparazzi... Okay. That's probably pushing it a bit, but some of your projects may indeed have the opportunity for significant life changes upon completion. What would success mean for your family? What would 'failure' on this mean for your family? These "team members" should absolutely have some say in the process or at least be informed throughout. Carefully considering those who will be impacted by your activities goes a long way to gaining their continued support.

Another stakeholder that I didn't fully consider was the audience for the book. Who was my audience? Where would they buy the book? What impact would I expect it to have on them? Although I had a good idea of who my audience was, I didn't actually sit down and write it out. I just started typing. Had I taken some additional time to solidify the audience, it would have served as a useful guide for my decisions and actions. Although it certainly impacts the writing itself, these decisions have a significant impact on promotion and marketing for sure. In business projects, these initial decisions are referenced throughout the design and implementation to keep that consistency of vision throughout. I have been on several projects where the team did not reference this initial charter or vision within each step. Suddenly a program was going to market in a way that didn't quite align with the original vision used for development. This misalignment can stop an initiative from being successful.

The big tag line in project management is, "You can have two but not three: fast, cheap, or good. In other words, you can have it fast and cheap, but quality will suffer. If you want a product fast, it can't also be high quality and cheap; you have to pick. In many cases, you're lucky to even get one. The role of the project manager is to help stakeholders identify what is most important and manage a plan toward that goal. Understanding the primary goals of the project will allow you to keep focus on what has been determined most important. If your top priorities are quality and cost, then you will need to add room in the schedule to allow for the extra time.

As you begin to build out your project plan, you can use expensive project management software, spreadsheets, or a notebook. Whichever route you go, be sure to keep it consistent. When I was first learning project management skills, I was told to use a specific piece of software. As a novice, it was completely overwhelming. There were so many rows, columns, drop-down boxes, and formulas, I didn't even know where to begin. Although I put my project in the fancy plan, I couldn't sort or run reports without spending hours learning the new software. Given my limited time (and interest in learning), I ended up copying it into my own simplified spreadsheet. Since it wasn't user-friendly for notes, I would take notes in a separate document or in my notebook, transfer them to the spreadsheet, and then put them in the fancy system when someone wanted to see the plan. I was a total mess. Eventually, I convinced the powers that be to just let me use my own system. As long as I provided the information they were interested in when they asked for it, I was finally permitted to use my own system, though it was forever referenced in my performance evaluation. After a bit of trial and error, I did eventually find a system that worked, and I still use it today.

Your system does not have to be fancy. Ultimately, you need to track the steps and information you need to be successful. If you are writing, perhaps you need to list out various drafts and due dates, return dates, resources you are going to use, and any budget items. If you are promoting a product, perhaps you need a bit more detail about sketches, samples, and revisions along with dates, resources, and budget. I keep it very simple with a list of tasks, dates, resources, and budget. If I am working on a larger project such as preparing for a conference, I may include categories with tasks underneath: speech writing, any additional content development needed, expo table materials, videography/photography, and travel. Depending on the size of the gig, I may not have a full project plan, but if I am working on something new, all of these pieces will need to be accomplished. I work much better with deadlines and activities I can check off. If I don't see it on the list, I will waste precious brainpower trying to recreate the list, documenting everything that comes to mind every time I think about the event. Some people can have a simple row in a spreadsheet with all of the items listed as column headers. I hope to get there one day. #Goals. The point I'm trying to make is that it doesn't have to be perfect, but start somewhere and be consistent.

When I first started working from home on my own projects, I failed to implement the timeline or deadline part of my planning. I thought I would just be highly motivated and not require deadlines. On the other side of the coin, I figured that my priority is to be with my boys, so I didn't really need deadlines. It would happen, and I was okay with that. Until I wasn't. Absolutely family is above work. I wholeheartedly believe that, and it is a primary reason for leaving the corporate world. I wanted to live my life on my terms, not someone else's. I carried that baggage with me and rejected everything that went along with feeling like I was at work. Ultimately, my relationship with my family suffered, my joy suffered, and my work suffered. I was feeling incomplete. After everything I did to get away from work, I was feeling unfulfilled because I wasn't striving. I was floating through my days with no real goals or sense of accomplishment. I did a lot of thinking but very little doing. When I started project planning my work, I felt a new fire inside of me and began to feel alive again.

If your work is important enough to think about, it is important enough to do, and do right! We were all given unique gifts and a unique mission here on earth. Until you are striving to fulfill that purpose, you will feel a little incomplete. Yes, kids are a *huge* part of that. Absolutely. And people are fulfilled every day by trying to be the best parent they can be. I have two brothers. I always wanted a sister, but that just wasn't in the cards for me. Fortunately, I have two very smart brothers who married two incredible ladies. I love them as if we have been together our entire lives. As close as we are, we couldn't be more different when it comes to our work/home situation. One of my sisters is a career woman through and through. She was on bed rest toward the end of both of her pregnancies and was just itching to get back to work by the time her leave was up. She loves her babies with everything she has, but she also has a need to wear heels, clothes without spit up, and a laptop bag. She is amazing at what she does and has worked her way into an awesome career. I couldn't be prouder of the woman, boss, and mom that she is.

My other sister has no desire to wear "real" clothes or sit behind a desk. She has two beautiful girls whom she homeschools, and she runs the household. For vacation money, she cleans houses for ladies at her church. As much as my brother and I have tried, we can't get her to show the slightest bit of interest in starting a cleaning "empire". She has no interest in building it and often gives her customers away when she has other community or church activities that keep her busy. Her time is spent with her family and community, and she is incredible at what she does.

As for me, I am somewhere in between. I have a strong desire to be with my boys, but I can't escape the pull of "something more". I just want to do it from home and on *my* schedule. People often frown when I say that, but two-thirds of you probably hear what I'm saying, even if you don't want to admit it. Believe me; I didn't want to admit it either. That's why I got stuck in the cycle I did. I felt guilty when I was working, I felt guilty when I was with my boys but thinking about my business, and I felt empty when I put my dreams on the backburner. Even though my boys filled my heart, I felt like I was letting myself down and forgetting who I was. It's hard to explain. Basically, I just felt guilty all of the time. Though I am always trying to be a better parent, I am also striving to be the best entrepreneur I can be. Some people are called to be awesome parents full-time. Some people are called to be awesome parents and awesome employees. Some people are called to be awesome parents and do a little something on the side. And all are wonderful. I encourage you to listen to the voice of desire inside of you. What is it that you feel passionately driven to do right now? If you aren't living in alignment with your calling and desires, then you will feel unfulfilled.

I will talk in the next section about organizing your time so that the feelings of guilt ease up. For now, I just wanted to highlight the importance of making a plan to achieve your goals and follow your dreams. If you don't, it is easy to keep pushing them off. When you do that, you are not at your best, which means your kids and family aren't getting your best. You all deserve better.

If I could describe myself in the safety of my closest friends and family without fear of having a future employer see and judge me by it, I would describe myself as a dreamer and a procrastinator. Often times, I use my gifts as a dreamer to fulfill my existence as a procrastinator. I would dream all day if given the opportunity. In fact, I am pretty proud of the fact that I can get more done in the 11th hour than in all the hours before; regardless of how many hours that is. I actually began to work this concept into my project plans and deadlines. Knowing that I worked best at the last minute, I would plan my day to be busy until the last minute so that I could get right to business and not waste time being unproductive beforehand. For years it made me very anxious that I couldn't get work done prior to the deadline. I would spend the days and hours before worrying and fretting over the fact that I couldn't focus until the last minute. Rather than being productive in other areas, I would solely focus on the fact that I was not being productive on that one project with the looming deadline. Although I made it work for me, this arrangement is absolutely not ideal. When it comes to your life, you want to be as efficient as possible with your time so you can spend it doing what you love most, *with* those you love most.

One way to do this more effectively is to set smaller, closer deadlines. Although it sounds obvious, a surprising number of us are really good at dreaming and setting goals, but we fail to put a time and date to it. I once heard that a goal is a dream with a deadline. Said another way, without a deadline, a goal is just a dream. Both of these sayings highlight the importance of establishing and maintaining a timeline with an actual deadline. This is where the idea of breaking goals down into smaller steps comes into play. A big goal or dream can often be too lofty. When there is always tomorrow, it is easy to put it off until there isn't a tomorrow. When the deadline is tonight, then you are more likely to accomplish it tonight. I can hear you all right now. "Duh. We know all of this." Yes, I know it too, but that doesn't mean I'm always good at it. Chances are, you aren't either. If you are like me, these big goals sometimes feel *too* big. I don't know quite where to begin or prioritize the wrong activities. Project managers help their project team prioritize by asking the question, "What is the very next thing you need to do to move the project forward?" Sometimes they even put together a Gantt Chart. These charts are designed to help project teams keep their priorities in order. Gantt Charts are linear representations of the project outlining each step in order. This before that; that before those. If a team member is working on a step that occurs much later in the process, it is the project manager's job to bring their attention back to the very next step in the process. Not the step that is the most fun, flashy, or easiest but the one that is next. Often, when we find ourselves avoiding a step, it is the very one that will move the needle on our goal. It is the very thing that you should be focusing on. By setting a deadline for yourself on each activity, every day, you are more likely to tackle those critical activities that propel you toward your goals.

Through the power of project planning, I was able to take those long-term, lofty dreams and turn them into smaller goals. I talked in the goal-setting section about taking big goals and breaking them down into smaller, more manageable goals such as a year, month, week, and day. This is a great way to see your goals in smaller increments, but the real power is in having deadlines. By having smaller, closer deadlines, your procrastinating spirit has less time to, well, procrastinate. When every day or every section of time has a deadline, it is always the 11th hour. When our next goal is not until the end of the month, it is easy to put action off. The mentality that, "there's always tomorrow" is a huge killer of dreams. There won't always be tomorrow, but even if there was, why would you want to wait?

Although project planning doesn't call for breaking goals and projects down to the daily level, it does add structure to your goals. From there, you can use your deadlines to build out the segments of your day and direct which activities you will focus on. If you need to write four blog posts a month, that equates to roughly one per week (remember there are approximately 4.5 weeks in a month…). What do you need to do each day in order to accomplish that? These guidelines will help push your progress along. I will talk more about building out your day in the next section.

The final point I'd like to make about the power of project management is reporting. Regular updates have benefits similar to the ones we discussed in the performance management portion. You must inspect what you expect. When a project gets assigned a project manager, resources, and oversight, you can bet that leadership will want regular updates on the progress. Pieces going well are highlighted in green while those with issues are yellow. When a project component is falling behind, it is highlighted red. The owner is called out, and everyone wants answers. Why is it behind? What do we need to do to get it back on track? What could you have done differently? I once stayed up two nights in a row to finish a piece of a project because we were having a project meeting, and I didn't want my piece to be red. It was a fairly arbitrary deadline and didn't impact the other team members, but there was a date, and I was going to meet it. Can you imagine how your own projects would progress if you had that kind of urgency behind your work? I'm not asking you to give up your health or critical time with family, but a few late evenings or a Saturday here and there to keep your dreams intact would sure go a long way, especially if you are enjoying a little more flexibility during the week (i.e., afternoon nap, morning trip to the park, the pool after school).

Sometimes we consider this a lack of balance. I truly believe "balance" is in the eye of the beholder. What is considered "balanced" differs from person to person. It also doesn't mean that I spend the same amount of time in each area of my life. To me, balance means that when I need to work a little harder, I can. When I have a little slack, I spend time with my boys. Ultimately you must make sure to swing the pendulum back and forth and not let it stick on one side for too long. That pendulum doesn't always swing with short strokes, though. Sometimes it swings really far to one side or the other. When you are in the middle of the "work" swing, it may feel like you don't have any balance at all. For women especially, it is more acceptable for us to spend more time on the family swing rather than the work swing. People are more likely to call you out when you are spending more hours at the desk but not necessarily the other way. We often internalize that and feel like in order to be balanced we must actually lean more on the family side than work. For some, that is balance. For others, the balance feels better on the work side. It doesn't always have to be a perfectly even balance between the two.

Additionally, at any given time, the pendulum is swinging to one side or the other. At that moment, that doesn't appear balanced. Eventually, the pendulum swings the other way, and for a moment, things appear to have evened out. As that pendulum hangs out for a moment, the balance again feels off. As the pendulum hangs on one side or the other, we often feel as if we are doing something wrong because, at the moment, there appears to be no offsetting swing. We begin to question our priorities and wonder why we can't figure this balance thing out. As I transitioned to a home office, I struggled to understand this balance. To achieve it, I sat with my boys as often as I could, but I was always working on something. I thought that by always doing both, I had achieved the elusive "balance". I quickly realized that by not focusing on one area at a time, I was actually not succeeding at either one. Most of all, I wasn't succeeding at "balance". The pendulum must swing both ways. It goes up, it hangs out a moment, then it swings back down. Balance does not rest in the moment between the two, it rests in the swinging back and forth.

Although the pendulum is intended to swing high on one end or the other, it is important to keep balance at the forefront of your mind. Make sure to include family time, rest, and relaxation. That doesn't always come naturally, especially if you are trying to achieve some big goals. Schedule time with family like you would any appointment, and protect it. I will talk more about this concept in future sections, but I wanted to touch on it briefly here.

Summary:

- Taking the time to outline your project charter is foundational for establishing a strong and effective project plan.

- Establishing timelines and deadlines for projects is key to reducing procrastination tendencies.

- We all need to be moving and growing to be fulfilled. Whatever that looks like for you, focus on moving forward in those areas.

TIME MANAGEMENT

Myth 15: I just need more time.

Truth 15: You just need to make better use of the time you have.

Oooh, how I dislike hearing this truth. It literally sends my head spinning. Okay. Not literally, but it has become such a com-back that we almost shame each other with it. Like somehow we are masters at making efficient use of our time or our job is to beat this truth into the lives of others. For years, I thought this phrase was merely suggesting that I work even faster and harder or that somehow these people preaching this truth were saying I was super slow. Working harder, faster, or giving up the things you love is actually *not* part of this truth at all. As much as it may make your hair stand up on the back of your neck, I encourage you to take a deep breath and with an open mind, let me walk you through this truth.

Whether it's an issue of procrastination or too many priorities, time management is often a topic of conversation. Although it might not come naturally, time management is a critical skill to master. Yes. I called it a skill. No one is born with incredible time management skills. It is something we have to learn how to do, and it's not something we are taught in school. Some people learn valuable skills and processes to retrain their brains to operate more efficiently, and some of us learn to work with our deficiencies while managing to somehow be productive through life. I have tried both ways, and I can tell you, learning to rewire your brain to function more effectively using time management practices is a much better way to go. I have actually taken several time management classes throughout my career. I fought implementing the techniques for years because I thought my way was better. I figured it wasn't worth the time and energy to practice and become proficient at new techniques. I just figured that was one way to do it and mine was another. Automating your decisions and behaviors essentially creates a habit, freeing your brain up for more "important" tasks. Once the process becomes automatic, it runs much more efficiently than the old way. Bottom line, it is worth the time to learn a new, faster way, even if it feels slower in the beginning.

One of the first things a time management training program will have you do is log your time for at least two days. Typically, you will have a sheet of paper with every hour of the day from about five or six in the morning until about nine or ten in the evening. Every hour will be broken down into fifteen or thirty-minute increments in which you document what you did during each increment. Some programs are more detailed and some broader, but this is the general gist. From there, you categorize your time. Categories vary but are intended to break your activities into time wasters, maintenance-type activities, income-producing activities, developmental activities, and family/recreation. You can also track your sleep, which is a nice touch.

The first two times I took a time management class, I blew right through this step. I thought I had a pretty good idea of where my time was going. I knew I was wasting time here, there, and around the corner, and I didn't need a log to tell me that. Needless to say, I did not take much away from those programs because I didn't have the baseline. After paying for two seminars and still struggling to be as productive and organized as I would like, I took a final seminar and decided to actually do the work.

I logged my activities for two full days in 15-minute increments. I could tell as I was writing in my activities that I was already noticing more time on "time wasters" than I thought. When I would get distracted, I would check my email, scroll through social media, flip on the TV, or read an article about a celebrity's new relationship. I knew I was wasting time, but I didn't really think it was *that* much; maybe five or six minutes here and there. What I discovered was that those five or six minutes was actually fifteen, thirty, or forty-five minutes at a time. When I did snap back quickly, I still got distracted within more fifteen-minute blocks than I thought. Over 25% of my productive fifteen-minute blocks had a distraction of some sort within it. When I get distracted, it takes me longer than the average seven or eight minutes to get back into what I was doing. Some research even suggests it takes twenty-five minutes to regain your focus after a distraction.[15] This is partly because jumping off of the hard task is easy. Switching back from the easy task is hard. This is certainly my experience, especially when I am writing or creating content. Even a simple knock at the door or ping on my phone can break my attention enough to completely derail my flow of thought. When you think about being distracted one or two times every hour or so, that is a lot of wasted time. I even got distracted at the mere thought of being distracted. I would pre-distract myself thinking, "Well, I probably only have about ten minutes, so there is no point in getting going." Thirty-five minutes later, and my "official" distraction had not yet called or arrived.

I cannot stress the importance of logging your day for at least two days. More will give you a better picture of how you spend your time. This log will give you a realistic picture of how much time you are *actually* spending in each category. Now, a log won't give you the complete picture of when you work best, but it will start to paint a picture. I color-coded my categories so I could more clearly see when I was most focused, when the kids needed me the most, and what I typically distracted myself with at what times. I had an idea about when I liked to work and when I felt most productive or creative, but I didn't really have any clear data around it. With my time log, I was able to marry reality with what I had in my head.

I found that I am most productive in the morning until about one o'clock, or until I stopped for lunch. My productivity picks back up again around seven in the evening and can continue until about two-thirty in the morning. After that, I lose it (as I imagine I should). I have done the time long now several times, which is how I have such a clear picture of my productivity. You likely won't get this off of one, two-day session, but you will gain some valuable insights for sure. Although my peak productivity and creativity hours are in generally the same order, since having children, they have shifted a bit due to competing priorities and sheer exhaustion. I don't expect you to pause and continue your time log before moving toward I do, though, encourage you to plan on conducting one and come back to this section. It will be significantly more meaningful once you have yours in front of you to reference.

So let's talk about how you use this data to maximize your productivity. Starting at the top, I learned that I am most productive first thing in the morning. Unfortunately, I was typically waking up with my alarm in just enough time to get to work before my boss noticed I wasn't there. Then I would spend the next hour visiting with colleagues and checking emails from the night before. I would spend my first couple of hours, my peak productivity hours, responding to emails from others. Now that I work from home, my day started with a pee-pee soaked pajama bottom in my face and the next two hours were spent chasing, feeding, and wrangling two little boys. When I did sit down at my computer, still during my peak performance hours, I would check email, catch up on any relevant gossip, and write out a very detailed to-do list complete with seventy-five critical items that I was going to get done that day.

As I was embarking on my first significant task, my phone would buzz, my email would ding, or an alert would announce that my utility bill was now available and due in twenty days. Each time I would stop what I was doing to look at the important distraction that just couldn't wait. That bill isn't due for twenty days, but if I don't schedule it right now, I'll forget about it. By the time I wrote in *schedule utility bill payment* just so I could scratch something off before noon, it was time to get lunch started. After lunch began my peak laziness hours, and I'm sure you can fill in the blanks for yourself. I was left wondering how in the world I could spend all day at my desk and not complete a single task that I could honestly say was propelling my business forward. That's when I dusted off my time log and brought back the techniques that I had implemented and helped others implement in my office.

I hear other moms and female entrepreneurs lament about not having enough time in the day. Entrepreneurs often end up working late into the night after the kids have gone to bed just to wake up at the crack of dawn with the kids. Meanwhile, other moms seem to *do it all*. Deep down we know they aren't as cool and collected as they seem, but there is no denying that some women get so much done while others struggle to fit it all in. I can tell you that no one can come close to doing it all without intentional action to make it happen. Just because it's important to you doesn't mean you have time to do it. You must consciously *make time*. This doesn't mean planting a seed of time and magically making time where there was none. When I say "make time", I mean cut something out and insert the important thing instead.

Taking care of a family is a full-time job. Whether you have a primary job, whether your kids are in daycare most of the time, whether you are a man or woman, whether or not you have help, it doesn't matter. It is a full time job to keep the house clean, maintain the household (pay bills, keep the appliances running, wait for the plumber, update the flooring, call about the extra charges on your cable bill, research a more reasonable phone company, cancel unused gym memberships....), provide your kids with their basic needs, provide them with the love and attention they really need, and have a fulfilling relationship with your spouse. Layer on personal goals like staying healthy, giving back to the community, having quiet time, relaxing, expanding your mind, and it is simply impossible to fit it all in. To think that this should come naturally is a myth.

Just because you don't naturally have time for it does not mean it isn't important or valuable. You can, though, do some things to make more time for the things that are important. We talked already about making a list of all of your tasks and eliminate or delegate those that you are uniquely equipped to do, you enjoy, *and* propel you toward your goal. Granted, you may not be able to delegate everything in the delegate column just yet, but by clearing off as many of these tasks as possible (and moving toward complete delegation and elimination of the list) you will find that your schedule begins to clear up. If you have not done that activity yet, stop now and go do it. I can tell you right now that you do *not* have time to do everything on that list. There is no point in trying to organize and Tetris something that just isn't going to happen. Even if you could fit it all in, your output and relationships would suffer.

So now that you have cleared off your activity list to those that are most critical and enjoyable, let's talk about how to schedule your day and organize your brain to make the best use of the time that you do have. My brain gets so active at night. As I'm trying to fall asleep, my brain goes through the day and all of the things I did or did not accomplish. Before I can shut it down, it's already working out my next day. I have a mental checklist that grows as my brain waves lengthen. Unfortunately, this mental activity often leaves me wide-eyed at two-thirty. The next day I would sit down at my desk and not know where to begin. I would spend a good part of my morning just figuring out where I left off the day before, identifying my next steps, and writing out a detailed to-do list, which I discussed earlier. For all the thinking I did the night before, it sure didn't help me when I needed to get into action.

How did I ever get anything done at work? What about before vacations or a weekend? A practice that project managers engage in is documenting notes at each meeting. Each team member would have to provide an account for where they were in the project, what the next step was, and the goal for the next meeting, which may be a week or two away. The project manager didn't have to remember where each project piece was; they simply looked at their project sheet. I had begun this practice for myself as well, and it changed my productivity at work. At the end of each day, I wrote a note about where I left off and what the next thing, or things, I was going to do for a given project. I would also write out my to-do list for the next day. This was particularly effective to do on Fridays, the day before a vacation, or before my maternity leave. It changed my mornings, and nights for that matter. Rather than staring blankly or roaming the halls for the first hour, I was actually eager to get to work because I had a plan and steps to take. I didn't flounder or fumble through notes, Word documents, or spreadsheets. It gave me new energy that started me off right and carried me through the morning.

What does your to-do list look like? Mine included everything from "do everything on this list", through "write a chapter", to "find someone to fix the roof before next fall". My list is ever-growing and is never in the same spot. I have notebooks, calendar inserts, calendar pages, sticky notes, and on-line apps. When I get bored, tired, or distracted, I start writing out to-do lists. I even found one tucked in the pages of my Bible the other day. I'm not proud of it, but I don't know that I'm completely alone here. We have too much to do. So when our to-do lists look like that, how do you know where to start?

The first step to regaining control of your day is to narrow down to or focus that list on those things that move the needle in the direction of your goals. Typically, there is only a small subset of activity that is critical now and fills that requirement. Exactly how many items/tasks that is, though, is often the subject of debate. Mary Kay Ash called it the six most important things list. Various others expanded that to include six most important things for your business, family, and home while others suggest there should be *only* six things on your list. Gary Keller and Jay Papasan in their book, *The ONE Thing*, instruct readers to identify the one (surprised?) thing that will propel you toward your goals today. Still, others suggest that identifying the top three things is all you should focus on because that is as far as you can focus.

I have never been able to narrow down my to-dos to just one thing, though I have benefited from the process of trying. On the other end, I find that having six most important things for every area of my life is equally overwhelming. I found myself creating areas of my life just so I could have more to-dos. I have been most successful keeping an ongoing to-do list on a calendar insert. I just move it through the pages of my calendar until I scratch them all off. Each day, I pull off the things that *must* get done today in order to propel your goals forward or move the needle in your life. I also take a look at things that I need to make progress on. Lack of urgency is the killer of progress. When things don't really *need* to be done, we move them down the list and can keep pushing them off for years. As we discussed in the goal-setting section, you must make smaller, shorter-term goals in order to create that sense of urgency. When something must get done, focus on those goals and the tasks associated with them. You may feel that making calls for a new hot water heater *must* get done today, and you might be right. When your priorities are based on those things instead of your goals, it can be easy to let the important, life-changing things slip through your fingers.

Whichever process works best for you, pick one and stick with it. Give it a chance to see if it works before pulling out and trying something new. Even businesses don't do this well, but it is one area where we can be *better* than they are. Businesses often give up right before an initiative is successful. As a Human Resources professional, I would caution you away from evaluating a process too soon. True change and benefit takes time. You have to let the shock of the change wear off before passing judgment. Employees and managers complain because they have to learn a new system or operate differently, and leadership often cancels before it has had a chance to work. With any change, there is an initial adjustment period. Give yourself time to learn a new way of thinking and a new system. Settle into it, give it a chance to work, and then determine if it's going to work for you.

Now that you have your list of the most important things that need to get done, let's talk about scheduling them. I don't know about you, but I love everything about a schedule. I even love the word *schedule*. *Schedule*. *Schedule*. *Schedule*. I could say it all day. I loved planning out my day and scheduling every single task on that schedule. I would have every line of a calendar filled up with activity. Whether it was an open box for the day, hour increments, or fifteen-minute increments, it didn't matter. I took my seventy-five critical item to-do list and began filling it in. It was like a little puzzle to see if I could get everything to fit. When I was done, I would feel like I had achieved something significant. "And they said there wasn't enough time in the day. Ha!" As much as I loved to schedule, I loved blowing through my schedule even more. Within the first thirty-minute block, I was already behind. I hadn't blocked time to schedule or *enough* time to schedule, and I certainly hadn't blocked time to surf social media *after* my scheduling. Since I was already behind, I may as well go ahead and make a snack so I could stay on track for the rest of the day. Once I had my snack, I would daydream about how awesome it would be if I could actually stick with my schedule and where I would be in five years if I just did this every day. Before I knew it, the day was over, and I would transfer everything back onto my to-do list for the next day. I thought detailed schedules were the way to go until I learned about something even better.

I had a co-worker whose calendar was always booked up. Lunch – blocked. First thing in the morning – blocked. Mid-afternoon – blocked. Four o'clock on Friday – blocked. How could she possibly be that busy? When I did find a hole in her calendar and snagged her for coffee, I asked what she was working on. She told me about her projects and all of the exciting things she was doing.

"Who is on your project team?" I asked.

"It's just me. I report to the steering committee." She responded.

"Do you have to meet a lot with other teams?" I continued.

"Occasionally, but not really." Before I could ask another question, she added, "Oh, but I did have lunch with Shannon from Marketing. Remember that gal we saw at the party? She introduced me to some folks, and I've had coffee with several of their team."

I couldn't believe that she had so much time to meet with other people. Her calendar was *always* blocked. How did she have time to have all of those meetings, meet with other people for "fun", and still get her work done?

"Debbie," I started, "how in the world do you have time to do all of this? Your calendar is *always* booked!"

Finally realizing what was bugging me the entire time, she laughed and said, "Girl, I block off my calendar to *work*! One of my goals was to learn about the different functions, so I block off time to do that too. In the morning, I work on my big project. I block off most mornings because I don't want to be distracted. I block off an hour every afternoon just to meet with people. If I'm not meeting with anyone, then I do work, but it is reserved for that. Three days a week I schedule my lunch to do yoga. I block off the first hour and the last hour just to check email and prepare for and wrap up the day. I schedule my time based on what's important. That way everyone else doesn't fill up my calendar with meetings so that I have to work all night just to get *my* work done."

"But, we work in cubicles. People don't interrupt you?" I just couldn't understand, logistically, how this worked.

"Oh yeah. If I *really* have to get something done, I book a conference room and go work there. Otherwise, we have these orange cones that we just put in our doorway. If someone sees the cone, they know that we're working and don't usually interrupt. It works really well. I don't know why we didn't think of that before!"

As odd as it sounds, I had honestly never heard of someone blocking off time to do actual work. In my mind, your calendar should always be available for people to schedule important meetings or to know if they can just pop in for a question. Therefore, my calendar looked like a checkerboard of meetings where there was hardly time to turn my laptop back on and remember what I was doing before it was time to head off to another meeting. I was scrambling all day and not allowing myself time for creative, thoughtful, productive work. The thought of networking or building relationships made me laugh because I didn't even have time to complete my tasks much less "chit chat". We talked more about what she did and the impact it had on her productivity and sanity. Aside from wanting to be more productive, I *really* wanted some of that sanity back. Since then, I have heard several different takes on this practice, but the principles are fairly similar across the board.

Tony Robbins refers to this type of organizing as "chunking". He discusses taking your day and chunking it into categories of time. Rather than identifying all of the unique activities you will do within that chunk, simply identify the type of activities. This could be working on your next blog post (writing, researching, brainstorming, seeking sponsors), household maintenance (calling the plumber, looking up a check that never got deposited, updating malware), or family (playing with kids, time with husband, helping with homework, snuggling on the couch). By identifying big chunks of time, you are able to do what you need to do, crossing a *lot* of things off of your to-do list or working on one important one. You can really focus on your work without being distracted.

This practice of breaking your day into chunks of time gives you a built-in sense of urgency. When you only have a limited amount of time to get the work done, you somehow manage to accomplish so much more. One day during the week I found myself with six whole hours all alone. Instead of being wildly productive as I imagined I would, I blew the entire day because I thought I had plenty of time to get things done. On the contrary, when I have only thirty minutes at my desk, I knock off half of my list. Parkinson's Law states that work expands to fill the time available for its completion. According to the chunking model, had I broken my day into blocks of time dedicated to specific tasks, I could have had several hours of productive thirty-minute blocks instead of a wide-open day of distractions.

There are various other productivity experts that have a similar approach to chunking. Across the board, the key take away is to put the important things on your calendar first before others get ahold of it. If your day is dictated by hair appointments, groomer visits, drop-ins, soccer practice, and random email requests, you lose the power that a big block of time can provide. Sure, you may need to schedule an emergency doctor visit during your protected time, but for the most part, you can schedule appointments during a specific block on your calendar. If you know when your productivity drops, schedule appointments or "coffee breaks" with friends for those times rather than allow their first opening to dictate your calendar. Often times, there are several options. By knowing when your time slot is, you can pick the time that works best for you without having any negative impact on them. As people begin to learn about your protected time, they will also learn to respect it. Again, it may be hard at first, but people will usually respect it if they understand it.

"But Cheryl," you may say, "my calendar is already full."

To that, I would reply, "Yes, I know." I believe your calendar is already full. I'm sure it is already spilling over, and that doesn't even include the things that you think you should be doing. We over-fill and over-schedule our time. Since I'm talking about scheduling your time, let's talk about what to schedule first. As you look at a blank calendar (not the one that's already full), schedule in the *big rocks*, those things that move the needle and have the greatest impact on your life. These things may include your business (schedule creative time separate from maintenance time), work if you have a j-o-b, family time, daily exercise and/or meditation, weekly lunch with mom, weekly coffee to network, and anything else you need to be most productive (i.e., an afternoon nap). Put those on your calendar first. We are creating an *ideal week*, so don't look back at your filled calendar yet.

I want to take a moment to talk a bit more about the significance of scheduling the important stuff on your calendar. When I was working in the corporate world, I imagined I would have such incredible balance when I finally was able to work from home. I imagined myself snuggled up to my desk hammering away for a few hours, taking a break to put in a load of laundry and play a game with my boys, then knocking out several more hours of work before shutting down for the evening and not thinking about it again until the next day. I visualized my life as a beautiful dance between home and work where the two lived harmoniously with very little fighting for attention. In reality, my work is always on my mind. When I'm with my boys, I am thinking about the unwritten words, unsent emails, and un-booked gigs. I'm afraid that if I don't slip in some work now, I might not get any time to do it. When I'm working, I hear my boys laughing and giggling on the other side of my door. I wonder why I'm so close but not enjoying any time with them. In the evenings I rush them off to bed to get a bit more work done, and in the mornings, I am trying to steal away a few moments to check email so I can "jump right in" to productive work when I get to my computer. My mind is always playing my endless to-do list and trying to figure out a short-cut to get me back in the game. Carving out specific time to do the important activities in your life will help you focus on the activity at hand. Knowing that you have three solid hours to work this afternoon, for example, will help you enjoy the two hours you spend with your children in the morning. Knowing you have scheduled time to take your kids to the pool after lunch will help you focus on work in the morning. You are giving yourself permission to focus on one without feeling as if you are taking time away from the other. This was a major game-changer for me.

Once you have the most important things on your calendar, think about the things you have to do or do regularly like appointments, meetings, and pick-ups. I'm not saying have to like we don't want to; these are just things that you know you need to plan for. If you pick up your kids or chauffeur them to practice in the afternoon, schedule it in. If it's something that you would rather delegate, then discuss that and get it off of your calendar. If you need or want to do it, then schedule it in. That way you won't be agitated and feel like that is taking away from your business time. This is scheduled, it is part of your day, and you can relax knowing that it all still works while you're enjoying time with your family. Schedule those times when you know you want to stroll into the kitchen and look for a snack. Turn it into a designated workout, appointment, or errand time. Just block off two to four, or whatever, for appointments/errands. When you need a hair appointment or your kid needs a physical for soccer, boom. "Tuesdays from two to four Mr. Scheduler sir. What do you have during that time?" Go to the appointment and get back on schedule. If you have nothing during that time, you can use it for household maintenance, read a book, or make-up work. The point is, you have scheduled time for those things that crop up and easily derail your productivity.

Would you like to see my ideal week? Well, I can tell you what it used to look like.

5:00 up

5:30 – 6:15 workout

6:30 – 7:00 dress

7:00 – 8:30 time with boys

9:00 – 2:00 j-o-b

2:00 – 6:00 write

6:00 – 7:30 dinner and family time

7:30 – 8:00 wind down

8:00 – 9:30 read, relax, and drift magically to sleep

Yeah, that's greeeeaaaat. That 5:30-6:15 slot never happened, but it was *always* on my calendar. The problem was my business time became a catch-all for home maintenance, meal planning, and rest. Therefore, if I wanted to make any progress on my business, I took it out of the night, and I never made it to that workout. I felt worse and worse every time I looked at it. If you realistically aren't going to do something, do not put it on your schedule. The last thing you need is for your calendar to criticize you every time you open it up. Create a calendar that works for you. I tried to implement the ideas of every productivity expert I could get my hands on.

The one I took most to heart was to block at least four hours of creative / work time in a chunk. Well, that is great coming from someone whose business *is* their j-o-b. For someone with a full- or part-time j-o-b in addition to their business and in addition to raising their family (not to mention those who also homeschool), it may not be realistic. Blocking creative time might be the easy part, but that may not move the needle on your business. Without actively making contacts and pitching your services, your creative efforts may just result in spinning your wheels. You may not have enough time to write for four hours and still maintain your business. I encourage you to understand the spirit of advice that you receive but ultimately do what works for you. It may take a few trials to find what works, but try to enjoy the process. The journey, after all, is what this life is all about.

I once outlined all of the things experts say we "should" be doing in a day. Including things like getting eight hours of sleep, working at least ten plus hours a week on your business, cooking and eating three meals a day at home, spending quality time with your spouse and kids, implementing a morning and evening ritual, reading for ten minutes, meditating, working out for the minimum, etc., we were over the time in the day not even counting the things that you need to do like driving places. Car needs to be registered? Whoops. Just take that out of your family time. You subscribed to a thirty-day trial that has now been charging your credit card for four months and you need to cancel? Take that out of your workout time. Rock cracked your windshield and you need to get the chip repaired before it splinters? Yeah. We're just going to take that out of your sleep. Because we still need to pick up the kids and make that appointment, these things end up pushing into our businesses, dreams, and self-care.

This is why it is so important to really narrow down your list of activities to those that are most important in your life and delegate or eliminate the rest. Can't get to mopping the floor this week? That's okay. Sandy will be here on Thursday. She'll take care of it. See how good that feels? Secondly, by chunking your time, you can just take care of that windshield between two and four when you have time scheduled for errands. Schedule a grocery pick-up instead or move that hair appointment to next week so you can take care of this "emergency". Do not reschedule your work time for this "emergency" if at all possible. If you do, you will look back a year from now and wonder how you didn't have any time to build your dream. I put *emergency* in quotes because a true emergency would absolutely take priority over your work. We do, though, term many things "emergencies" that really aren't. I encourage you to truly evaluate the situation and determine if it can wait until your scheduled time to address such issues.

In organizations, these situations are often called "fires". Someone is always "putting out a fire". The reality is, if you let them, people will always pull you off of your work for theirs. Their emergency becomes yours. I had a co-worker who would regularly say, "Lack of planning on your part does not constitute an emergency on mine." I thought he was a little harsh and inflexible, but now I totally get it and appreciate his stand. This also allowed him to properly focus on others who equally deserved his time.

This leads me to the third and final takeaway in this section. As much as we have talked about blocking your time, if you don't respect the blocks, then it doesn't work. I'm not just talking about protecting your time from others, which is critical, but I am also referring to protecting it from yourself. It is so easy to say, "Just this once" or "I'll just do this really quickly", but once you start cutting into your blocks of time, you break down your self-integrity. Keeping those self-promises and valuing your time is essential to self-esteem. Once you start protecting your time, you will find yourself more productive and focused during that time because your brain doesn't have the *option* to become distracted. You build that habit of focus, and it becomes second-nature. Additionally, others will begin to respect your time as well. You have to *teach* yourself and others to respect your time.

Once I started blocking my time, it was like I put blinders on my mind. I scheduled my time, protected it, and enjoyed it. I knew I would have enough time to get enough work done today, so I could enjoy the time I was spending somewhere else. Rather than trying to fit in four hours of focused work in tiny snippets, always chasing it when I should be thinking about something else, it was reserved on my calendar. I knew it was there, so I could stop worrying about it. When I did sit down to work, I knew that I would be playing with my boys again in a few hours. That allowed my brain to rest, shut that door, and focus on the work at hand. I became more focused and a lot more fun to be around. I also let go of some of the guilt that said I wasn't spending enough focused time with my boys. Although I was *with* them a lot, I was often thinking about something else, and that's if I wasn't physically *doing* something else while with them. By scheduling and protecting your time in this way, it will free up your mind, body, and spirit to be more productive and engaged in your life. As much as you need to schedule time for your own sanity, your kids need to know when they will see you. They need to know that mommy is working right now but will be able to play later. And when you *are* playing, you are 100% present. I want you to be there and really experience your life, not just get through it

Summary:

- Realistically schedule your day. Schedule time to work, play, relax, and run errands. Book activities within those dedicated blocks.

- Respect and protect your time. If you don't respect it, no one else will.

- Blocking or chunking your time creates a sense of urgency to accomplish tasks and a sense of peace to enjoy doing things you truly enjoy.

BURNOUT

Myth 16: You can't experience burnout doing something you love.

Truth 16: If you do anything without the proper rest and rejuvenation, including living your life's passion, you will burn out.

When a mom is discussing her level of exhaustion with another mom, she often begins or ends it with, "but I really do love my kids", as if she thinks we believe that being completely wiped out and in need of a break somehow means she doesn't love her children. I hear this same idea come across when women talk about their j-o-bs or businesses. "But I really do love what I do". It breaks my heart that we feel that we need to qualify our exhaustion by reminding others that we don't hate our lives. I want to shout from the rooftops: You can love your life and still need a break! You can do what you love and still be tired. You can do what you love and still get excited about taking a break. Believe it or not, you can do what you love and still experience burnout. It is okay and completely normal to need a break from time to time. Even machines need to recharge every now and then.

I want to take a moment to really understand what burnout is all about. As I discussed earlier with the term "love", we often use the term burnout to describe a temporary state of being tired of your job or frustrated with your boss. It goes beyond a bad day or even a bad week. Just the other day, my friend recently asked me, "Do you ever have those days when you just don't want to parent?" My answer was, "Yes. Yes, I do. In fact, I may be having one right now." I have my boys in a Mother's Day Out program on Tuesdays and Thursdays. After having them at home Friday through Monday, I can't get them to the church fast enough come Tuesday morning. I didn't love my boys any less on Tuesday mornings when I was worn out, but I was certainly a better mom come Thursday afternoon after having a little break. When your energy and enthusiasm ebbs and flows consistently or routinely, you are likely experiencing something more along the lines of tiredness rather than true burnout. Do not read that to say you need to power through it and not give yourself a break. You are still perfectly capable of having a mental breakdown and need to step back. This is simply a slightly different topic than what I am discussing in this section.

Additionally, I want to reiterate that depression may also show symptoms similar to burnout. Although the symptoms may be similar, the cause of clinical depression is often an imbalance in neurochemicals in the brain. Chronic burnout and stress can drive some of this imbalance, but it will be much more effective to address the imbalance directly. As I discussed previously, if you believe you may be suffering from depression, I encourage you to seek professional help while also continuing to better understand whether or not burnout may be a contributing factor.

Now that we understand what burnout is not, I would like to take a moment to better understand exactly what burnout is. Christine Louise Hohlbaum, author of *The Power of Slow: 101 Ways to Save Time in Our 24/7 World*, describes burnout as the "slow-creeping syndrome" and "silent condition" induced by chronic stress characterized by emotional or physical exhaustion, cynicism, and lack of professional efficacy.[16] Professional efficacy may not be a term you are familiar with, but it is similar to the imposter syndrome we talked about earlier. It is your overall belief in your own professional abilities and the sense that your professional activities produce some kind of desirable or beneficial result. In this sense, in addition to leaving you chronically exhausted and fairly negative about the world in general, burnout causes you to begin to doubt yourself, your abilities, and your purpose. It sneaks up on you, especially when you aren't paying attention to your body, spirit, and mind.

The term "burnout" was coined in 1974 by psychoanalyst Herbert J. Freudenberger. He defined burnout as "the extinction of motivation".[17] Psychologist Christina Maslach further discovered that burnout results from a misalignment between our lives and our belief system.[17] Our actions and beliefs must be in harmony. Our workload alone, for example, isn't enough to cause burnout, but when it interferes with our sense of control, reward, community, sense of fairness, and values, it becomes a burden rather than a source of joy and fulfillment. I will dig into this a bit more in this section, but I want to draw your attention to the connection with meaning and values. We discussed these factors and their role in engagement. Although you may still grow tired and need periodic breaks, engagement is a significant factor in reducing burnout. When your work is aligned with your needs and values, when you experience significant meaning from your work, you are less likely to experience true burnout.

Although burnout is "slow creeping", it is accompanied by a number of clues or symptoms. Unfortunately, we often overlook them. We push them down, justifying with, "Oh, I'm just tired today," or "I just have this big project coming up. I'll be fine after that". With obligations for children, trying to maintain a strong marriage, building a business, maintaining a j-o-b and/or household, and trying to fit in a social life, it's no wonder that maintaining our sanity is often the first to go. We ignore that tiny little voice that says, "Slow down!" We "buck up" and just keep pushing when our bodies need to rest. We take on one more project when we are already overbooked. After we let ourselves go, the next to suffer is often our families, our social lives, and then things start spiraling out of control. When we aren't getting to be with the people and do the things that are driving our desire to build a business in the first place, we start to wonder what it's all about. What is this all for anyway? You may suddenly crash on the couch, have a mental block, find that you have lost meaning and joy in your work, or find yourself in the hospital. Although the final straw is often sudden and harsh, the warning signs are typically soft and persistent.

In her research, Hohlbaum[16] shares some questions to ask yourself to help identify whether or not you may be suffering from burnout. If you feel that you may be suffering from burnout, I encourage you to pause a moment and reflect on the answers to these questions.

Are you starting not to care about work anymore?

Is it hard to stay motivated?

Do you feel your workplace is a dreaded place to be?

Are you snapping at your colleagues?

Do you feel disengaged from your work?

Have you lost your passion for things?

You may not be experiencing full-on burnout yet, but perhaps you are beginning to experience withdrawal symptoms. These symptoms can last years, but inevitably, they will lead to burnout if you don't do something about it. We talked earlier about the myth that when you love what you do, you will never again work a day in your life. You can absolutely love what you do and still experience burnout. It may take longer than it does when you are doing something you aren't passionate about, but it still happens. And this doesn't just happen with work. You can burn yourself out of your children as well. In these cases, there are some things you can do to maintain your sanity on an on-going basis and not just when you are about to crack. Hohlbaum suggests making time for yourself daily through simple tasks like taking a brisk five-minute walk to the mailbox and back, grabbing your favorite cup of coffee or allowing one entire hour of uninterrupted time to "just be".[16] Just be. I love that idea, but man is that hard. What would I do if I was to just be? No guilt, no responsibility, no tasks. An entire hour may feel overwhelming at first, and I get anxious just thinking about being intentionally unproductive for an entire hour, but it can be any amount of time that you determine. If you can't just be, then read a book, do a Sudoku puzzle, or color in one of those adult coloring books. I like the brainless activities like coloring because it allows your brain to wander and meander. As beneficial as a walk is for your body, a mental meander is rejuvenating for your mind. In this way, it is similar to meditation. This downtime is so crucial to having a successful business and meaningful life

They don't always do a great job of it, but companies are beginning to see the benefit of taking care of their employees and encouraging them to step away from work at the end of the day and take allotted vacation time. Some organizations are even going to far as to offer unlimited vacation. Organizations have begun referring to this as PTO (paid time off) rather than "vacation" and are including vacation, sick time, and holiday time. If given their way, most companies would work their employees 24/7, so the fact that there is a trend away from this behavior suggests strong research pointing to the monetary benefit of time away. As we have been discussing throughout this book, we often fail to see ourselves as an asset or employee in need of a break. When we are pursuing our passion, we believe that we somehow step into an alternate universe where energy is infinite and rest unnecessary. If we can just find that passion, we can tap into energy stores the rest of the world doesn't experience. Instead of taking a break, we push ourselves to the breaking point in the name of "entrepreneurship". It is true to a certain extent that we tap into extra energy when pursuing meaning and purpose, but even our God-given energy stores need rest.

Although burnout is a very real issue, it is not inevitable. If you are aware of the warning signs and in tune with your body, mind, and spirit, you can stop burnout and reverse its effects. In her book, Hohlbaum suggests tips for preventing burnout from settling in and taking hold of you.[16] First of all, she says, to "recognize when your passion has turned to poison. If you no longer wake up with fire in your belly – but rather with your stomach on fire – you are burned out." It's one thing to feel anxious about a project, deadline, or finances; it's another to feel burdened by your work or family. If it is pulling you away from the most important things too much, then it can become burdensome and heavy. Hohlbaum also discusses how burnout can lead to isolation. This is one form of withdrawal, which is a noted sign of burnout. You may be too physically *or* emotionally exhausted to engage with family or friends. The more burned out you are, the more energy it takes to focus on and push through your work. Rather than being engaging and experiencing flow, every email, every word is a burden. That constant push takes a physical, mental, and emotional toll on your body making it hard to get excited about being around other people. If you find yourself pulling away from people and activities you once enjoyed, evaluate the reason. Withdrawal and isolation can lead to depression, which creates a difficult circle to get out of.

If you find yourself beginning to show signs of burnout or withdrawal, take some time to honestly assess your situation. Are you feeling the temporary, good exhaustion that accompanies passionately pursuing your dreams, or have you moved to a point where pursuing that passion has become tiring? Do you still feel connected to your mission and purpose, or do you no longer feel alignment between your work and your values? I encourage you to take some time to rest and reflect on your business and purpose. Reflect on your family and your *why*. Reflect on what success means to you and how you are walking in obedience. This time of reflection is not simply a bubble bath or a night away. Yes, we need to do those things to maintain our sanity and continue to push forward. If you are truly experiencing burnout, these breaks will only provide temporary relief. That nagging, aching exhaustion and cynicism will continue to haunt you until you identify the source of misalignment and find the resolution.

During your extended period of rest and reflection, ask yourself the following questions:

What am I passionate about?

Am I doing those things?

Why am I doing what I am doing?

What would I feel if I were to change my situation?

What one thing can I change today?

What action can I take to alter my position? Can I allow myself to take a break from my current situation?

How long would I need?

If you have found yourself in a state of burnout, you may need to take more extreme measures to combat your state immediately. We talked earlier about cutting out tasks that you aren't uniquely equipped to do, that you aren't passionate about, and don't move the needle of your life. Those tasks you are doing outside of that can be a significant contributor to burnout. Go back to that list and see if there are things you are doing that you don't need to do. If so, find a way to eliminate, delegate, or automate those activities. Similarly, as people make requests of you, it will be crucial to learn the *skill* of saying "no". Skill? Yes. Learning to say "no" is a skill and a critical one to master. Particularly for people-pleasers like myself (that is not the great compliment I always thought it was), it is easy to find yourself with a life dictated by the requests and expectations of others. We want to make everyone happy or just don't want to have a confrontation, so we take on this, that, and the other. Before long, we find ourselves pulled in 80 different directions. We may not be burned out by our work, but that's only because we haven't actually *touched* our work. In reality, we are burned out by everything else, but the stress of not doing what you know you should be doing leads to additional stress, and it all gets lumped together.

Using the word "should" in the previous paragraph brings me to a quick detour to discuss cognitive dissonance. I have talked a great deal about the alignment of your work to your values, desires, and purpose, and you may be wondering why I harp on that so much and how it impacts burnout. Perhaps you have taken a psychology course or read a book that discussed the term cognitive dissonance. It is a basic principle in Psychology 101 and in my opinion, doesn't ever get the time it deserves. Cognitive dissonance is the internal struggle we experience when our actions don't align with our beliefs. Simply stated, when we use the term "should" but aren't doing it, we experience cognitive dissonance. Even if we aren't aware of the struggle, our brains are. When someone says, "I really *shouldn't* eat this muffin," and then proceeds to eat it, they may think nothing of it. Their brain, on the other hand, says, "Whoa. You just said you *shouldn't* eat that. But you ate it. What's going on? Do we eat muffins? I thought we didn't eat muffins. We aren't "supposed" to eat muffins, but we do it anyway. I guess we just don't do what we're "supposed" to do. Healthy people don't eat muffins, but we're not healthy. Why are we eating this muffin? We know better than this. We never do what we know we should do. We just can't do anything right. We'll never be able to resist that muffin. If we were healthy, this wouldn't be a problem." And on, and on, and on. With every bite of the muffin, the brain struggles with whether or not we should be eating the muffin. It was an innocent comment and one we have all made, but the damage it's doing internally goes far beyond the 200 calorie decision we *thought* we were making.

As we continue to not do things we believe we *should* do, this language gets stronger and stronger. In order to ease the argument inside, we begin to convince ourselves it isn't really that important. "I don't really want to start my own business." "I am happy at this weight." "My marriage is good enough." We begin to settle for mediocrity because that's what our actions are saying we want. Our brains are trying to make sense of everything, and actions outweigh thoughts and desires. Yet as hard as our brain tries, it just can't quiet that voice inside that says, "I *do* want more." It's that voice that comes from our heart and spirit. Despite our confusing actions, our heart knows where we belong. It knows our purpose and holds that drive that we have convinced ourselves we don't have. The longer we ignore it, the more it pulls and tugs. Our brains are so powerful. Our actions become habits, and they become part of our subconscious mind. As I said before, that part of our brain processes information at 400 billion pieces of data (bits) per second. As our actions become habits, we don't even have a chance to think about them. We just grab the muffin or scroll through social media. The slower part of our brain, our consciousness, doesn't even have time to stop the behavior before we're in it. Processing information at only 40 pieces of data (bits) per second, it's still trying to catch up. "What just happened??" It just doesn't have the "brainpower" to stop these habits without conscious effort to do so. Meanwhile, our heart is crying out in muffled spurts. "Remember your dream." "Don't give up." "You can do it!" Our spirit hears it, but our brain ignores it. Over time, we get better and better at convincing ourselves that we don't want it or need it. Although we may learn to avoid the inner turmoil and overcome the resulting burnout (though I don't believe we ever really do), the greater travesty is not living up to your God-given potential in this lifetime. Your children miss the opportunity to see you strive and achieve, your spouse misses the opportunity to support you, and those impacted by your work lose the opportunity to be touched by your efforts.

I encourage you to take a moment to listen to your heart. What is it saying? What dreams have you stuffed behind broken *shoulds*? What have you convinced yourself that you don't need or want because it was too painful to not have it? What did you decide wasn't worth striving for? Once you have had that conversation with your heart, I ask you to identify those broken *shoulds* that are keeping you from achieving those dreams. Where did it all go wrong and what can you do today, right now, to start moving those behaviors from habits to conscious decisions? It won't be easy to undo those habits that have been engrained over years or decades, but it is an important step in moving toward a life of intentionality and alleviating the turmoil caused by cognitive dissonance.

Summary:

- Burnout is an overwhelming sense of exhaustion, cynicism, and lack of faith in your abilities and purpose.

- Symptoms of burnout include withdrawal, exhaustion, and lack of motivation.

- You can reduce the symptoms of burnout by evaluating your actions and re-establishing your *why*.

LEADER DEVELOPMENT

Myth 17: I'm not a leader.

Truth 17: You are a leader....or should be.

A while back, a professional athlete was publically criticized for his bad behavior off the court. Fans were upset because they said he was being a poor role model. He retaliated with, "I never asked to be a role model." The resounding response was, "You don't have a choice." When you are in the public eye or spotlight like professional athletes and celebrities, you don't have a choice as to whether or not you are a role model. The choice you *do* have is whether or not you are going to be a good one or a bad one.

Women across the board tend to struggle with the idea of being a leader. We often don't see ourselves in that role either because of a lack of confidence/self-esteem or because we are uncomfortable thinking of ourselves in a raised position. To address the latter, in most corporate, hierarchical environments, leaders are considered *above* their teams. A CEO is the "head" of the organization. They are seen as authority figures, but the position also comes with a certain amount of respect and admiration. Furthermore, leadership is often viewed as a position. More and more organizations are recognizing the idea of leaderless workgroups and teams where "leadership" rotates among the team members based on the project or expertise. Ultimately there is always someone who has approval rights, etc., but the idea is to de-elevate the idea of a leader. More commonly, organizations are requiring leaders to be more visible and accessible. In one organization, the CEO got rid of the executive cafeteria and made all of the top leaders use the cafeteria with the rest of us. For a while, no one really knew what to do or how to act. Over time, they became less of a figure and more of a team member. Lines of communication that hadn't been opened previously became well-traveled highways. Executives had a greater understanding of their workforce needs and struggles. They began to appreciate what their employees were bringing to the table because they got to know them on a different level. They overheard conversations, had impromptu discussions, and met employees they had interacted with only virtually in the past. When leaders become people and less of a voice behind the curtain that is when things really start to happen.

Regardless of their approach, organizations are beginning to recognize the role leaders play across and within the organization. Within work teams, a leader often emerges to provide guidance to the team. As moms, we often struggle with stepping into this role, whether formally assigned or informal, but we are leaders none the less. Our children look up to us for guidance, direction, and discipline. We make financial, health, spiritual, educational, and recreational decisions. We set the tone for the day and beyond. We also serve an informal role in influencing other adults in our households. Have you heard the phrase, "if momma ain't happy ain't nobody happy"? Just like a leader in an organization, you set the tone for your families. You have more influence over them than you think, and this is an important role you play. Just like the professional athletes, you are a role model. You only need to decide if you are going to be a good one or a bad one. If you are running a business with contractors, vendors, employees, customers, and/or a team of volunteers, you are a leader. You are also leading future buyers to buy your product. You are indeed a leader, and leadership skills don't always come naturally. Organizations invest hundreds of thousands of dollars annually building their leadership skills. These numbers are my best estimate based on my experience working with these large organization, but the takeaway is, organizations carefully groom people to become leaders and spend a significant amount of money evaluating and selecting the best leaders, and those *very* leaders are often the ones directly responsible for destroying a culture or bringing an organization down.

Often leaders try to implement change within their organization, like the culture change we discussed at the beginning of this book. Despite their best efforts, it often takes time for an organization to show signs of change. We face these same struggles at home. As we try to change the landscape for our families, we often face resistance or slow change. In these times, it is important to remember your values, purpose, and definition of success. If you have taken the time to carefully and prayerfully consider the direction for your family, you must have faith that the change will come. Persistently pursue your path until you hear otherwise.

One approach organizations have begun to take in preparing leaders for success is to outline a 100-day roadmap. Rather than coming in and immediately making changes (though it often feels like that is exactly what they're doing), leaders are instructed to spend the first 100 days in their new role talking, observing, and planning. They talk to leaders and team members in various parts of the business. They learn about the pain points and hear ideas from others. Only after they have completed a thorough analysis of the business do they begin making significant changes. Not only is this critical for making sound decisions, but it also goes a long way to gaining buy-in from the organization. When a leader has personally visited with you or has taken the time to learn about your needs, it is hard not to feel the tug of support. This 100-day plan has become an essential part of executive leadership onboarding and ramp-up in many organizations. If the highest-paid executives take time to learn the lay of the land and build relationships, then we should not feel guilty doing the same.

Many of us have felt the pain of working with a leader who was promoted before they were ready. Many organizations take someone who is *really* good at what they do and promote them to a manager, director, and beyond. Just because someone is technically skilled does not mean they have the ability to manage an individual or team. Organizations are becoming aware of this gap and pursuing development programs geared toward preparing leaders for leading people as well as develop them throughout their journey. Where we once promoted a leader and left them to fend for themselves, driving off high potential employees along the way, we now prepare them with the skills they need to be successful. I don't know about you, but I don't know too many women who have taken a class on becoming a mom or took a course in running a business prior to jumping in. Instead, we figure that we are smart, skilled elsewhere, and can *figure it out*. Surprisingly, most of us are pretty successful despite the lack of continuous education, but the reality is, we could be so much better! This is important for our work but also for adding some sanity back to what you do.

We often understand the benefit of continuous education in terms of attending conferences or seminars on our primary topic or mode of delivery (i.e., substance abuse or blogging). We can understand that research is continually evolving and bringing new ideas and techniques to light. If we want to be successful, we must be on the front edge of these advancements.

One thing individuals and organizations alike often overlook is the importance of soft skills. I touched on soft skills a bit throughout this book, and I want to bring it back for a moment here. Technical skills are those skills that specifically relate to the specific tasks of the job. Therefore, they have a great deal of face validity. Someone can look at the skill and clearly see the connection to the job. Soft skills, on the other hand, don't always have an obvious and immediate impact, which makes it hard to calculate Return on Investment. If you can't calculate Return On Investment, organizations will move on to the next big thing.

I have no doubt that you have more natural leadership ability than many of the highest-paid executives in American corporations, but I also have no doubt that there is room for improvement. Soft skills can indeed be developed, though it is a more difficult process than developing technical skills. It takes time and energy to cultivate a leadership style that works for you and those you lead. Even independent business owners need to take time to develop their skills. Read articles on leadership in the area of interest for you. Perhaps that is parenting skills or teaching. Maybe you are indeed leading a team or want to lead people to your product (i.e., marketing or sales). By developing your leadership skills, you can learn techniques and strategies for leading your team through life's toughest challenges, and I'm not referring only to your business challenges here.

Summary:

- Whether you see yourself as one or not, you are a leader.

- Leadership doesn't always come naturally. It is critical to take time to develop those skills just as you would in any other important area of your life.

- Spend more time developing soft skills than technical skills.

SUCCESSION PLANNING

Myth 18: When it comes to who will take over my business, I can cross that bridge when I get there.

Truth 18: When you get there, it will probably be too late.

Many organizations don't think enough about their plan for transition or succession until after it's too late. When the founder, leader, head, or CEO mentions they are thinking about retirement, suddenly the lightbulb goes off. "Who's going to take over?" And this doesn't just apply to the leader of the entire organization. Functional, regional, or any critical leadership roles should have a succession plan. The reality is, we need to start thinking about this long before leadership is ready to move out. It takes time to ramp someone up, even if they have been in or around the organization a while. When that leadership is you, and you have visions of spending more time with the grandkids or sipping a cocktail on the beach, that is the time to *execute* the plan, not *write* the plan. If it's important enough for you to spend your precious time and energy on now, it's important enough for you to think through a plan to help ensure it lives on long after you're enjoying retirement, even if the retirement is just from *that* business.

Perhaps you believe your children are going to want to take over when you are ready to retire, or perhaps you haven't begun thinking about it at all. Whether or not you believe your business needs a succession plan, there are some things you should at minim consider. It can be as simple as outlining a plan for dissolving the business or as complex as the logistics of who will take over, how, and when. It can even include a contract as to how things will operate moving forward. It certainly does not have to be too complex at first, but it is critical to begin thinking through your desires, the interests of others, and the ultimate goal of the work you are doing. Operating without having considered the future is like heading out on vacation without even a rough sketch. Sure, it can be exciting, but you're likely to get stuck paying too much for a trashy hotel, you may miss something incredible just an hour away, and it could end up ruining the entire vacation. Just a little planning could be the difference between running out of gas in the middle of Death Valley or having an incredible trip. All I'm asking is that you book a few hotels, map out your general route, and take out enough cash in case you get stranded. That doesn't sound so hard, does it?

Succession planning is just a fancy way of answering the question of who is going to take over next. In organizations, this could be examining the pipeline of talent moving up through the organization and across the various functions. It could also be determining the plan for replacing the executive leadership team or critical functions. It is always exciting to watch someone being "groomed" for executive leadership. Most notable is the plan to replace the CEO or President. People definitely act a little different toward that person once they are in line for CEO. I had a colleague who didn't realize that her team's executive was actually someone in line for the CEO position. Her team welcomed new employees by filling their cubicle with snacks so everyone would stop by, grab a snack, and say "hi". The executive stopped for a donut and to chat a minute. As he entered, he made a comment about the donuts as he grabbed one. Being a little awkward in general, she patted his tummy and jokingly said, "It looks like you've already had enough". He chuckled, not yet sure of her humor. It didn't take long for her to learn that he was expected to be the next CEO. She immediately remembered her initial interaction with him and was pretty sure he too thought about it every time he saw her. I can totally see myself doing that, and it makes me smile every time I think about it. People *love* to be among the "chosen ones", and they typically begin acting a little more professional when they are around. I don't recommend patting anyone's belly like a Buddha, but it does make for a good (however irrelevant) story.

Although I talk quite a bit in terms of organizations and businesses, important causes, non-profits, blogs, or families can benefit from these plans as well. I often think about how my boys would be raised if something were to happen to me. How will my husband make the transition to running the household and finances if it was suddenly dumped in his lap? If you are struggling to consider your business or cause worthy of a succession plan at the moment, practice these techniques with your family first and move on after you've gotten the hang of it and recognize the value.

One of the most important considerations in succession planning is the transfer of knowledge. When someone leaves an organization, it is customary to give at least a two-week notice. Although this is often thought of as an opportunity for the organization to find a replacement, rarely can a suitable replacement be found within two weeks. That time, though, is incredibly valuable for transferring their years of knowledge or expertise to the team or the person taking their place. Without this critical step, important processes could be disrupted.

In your family or business, there is likely a rather significant amount of knowledge you hold. You probably don't even realize it, but simple things like email passwords, bank accounts, and log-in information can make it challenging for someone to take over or even move on if you were suddenly out of the picture. I know none of us want to even think about this, but the reality is, there will be pieces that must be picked up, and someone is going to be left doing it.

Although you may not be thinking about it right now, preparing for an emergency situation or even the traditional business transfer early will make the process much smoother for you or those you care about. Begin thinking through what knowledge will need to be transferred and what that process looks like.

Many organizations create process maps to detail critical activities. This activity serves to add consistency to how the process is completed by different members of the organization, but it also serves the purpose of transferring knowledge to the next person. Detailed steps make the transition significantly smoother and save you from having to outline it all when you are mentally wearing your flip flops and grandma-appropriate swimsuit. By starting the process early, you will have a smoother and more successful transition.

In addition to knowledge transfer, it is important to think through the critical tools and systems you use in your family or business. Can these systems, programs, websites, social media pages, etc. be transferred? For my books, I use a program for all of my research and the building of my content. If something were to happen to me, without knowledge of the program and log-in information, my family would have a difficult time finding all of the incredible manuscripts I have just hanging out in that program waiting to be discovered and published posthumously. In all seriousness though, there are systems that will need to be transferred or at least have that ability. Take time to make a list of those systems, confirm that they are transferrable or at minimum the content accessible, and document account information for easy access later.

Another piece of the data transfer puzzle is the administrative side of the organization. This includes things like finances, vendors, employees, payroll, relevant historical knowledge, and all the ins and outs of running the business itself. How and when do we ship orders? Who creates our products? How do our employees/vendors get paid? Who does our taxes? Do we have customer service? Am *I* customer service? A great way to start detailing this information is to just go through your day. Any organizational process or administrative responsibility that you touch, interact with, answer questions about, or lead, write it down. This will be a critical piece of information for your succession plan. Not only will this make it easier for someone to take over if you need to, ahem, step out quickly, but it will also be an important thing to begin delegating to someone learning the organization for the purpose of serving as your replacement.

So far we have talked about things that can be transferred fairly easily through process mapping or simply writing a few notes in a folder. With any family or small business, there are things that are less easily transferred and take time to develop, acquire, or buy into. If you have the time, developing someone to take your place is the best way to implement a succession plan, though you always want to have a backup plan for that person as well. People have minds, and they like to change them. A child, family member, friend, or colleague may have big plans of taking over one day, but they can't always see into the future. If they win the lottery and take to the beach early, what's your backup? This is *your* business. Putting too much faith in a mere mortal who may not have the same passion you do is risky business. Organizations never have their eyes on a single successor for a position. They are constantly scanning the field to see what new talent is moving up, how the business is changing, and whether or not the pipeline they are creating is still in alignment with the organizational goals. Your business is no different. Succession planning is not a one-and-done event. It is a process of refinement until you have officially passed the torch.

Technical knowledge is one of those areas that takes time to develop. Organizations typically look for someone with foundational technical knowledge, but they take it upon themselves to *teach* them what they need to know or help them *acquire* that knowledge over time. We talked earlier about soft skills and values. These are less trainable qualities and ones that organizations have begun to hire for over the previously crowned technical expertise. The idea is that they hire for the tough stuff and teach the rest. Your business may be similar. The more critical technical skills are in your business, the earlier you need to start your succession planning process. If you wait until the last minute, you are going to end up seeking out the technical side at the cost of the more important characteristics like values. It will be difficult to find someone with the right balance of both. Starting early allows you the opportunity to *develop* technical skills over time.

This is the way organizations operate. As they "groom" their leaders, they rotate them through the functions to gain the technical knowledge of the different departments. This is why Human Resources functions often have executive leaders who don't actually have any HR background. The field is important enough to gain experience, but the real expertise sits in the seats of the worker bees. Although the leader will likely not be asked to perform any specific technical *activity*, having broad technical *knowledge* allows them to perform better in their future roles. The technical side is developed over time and is rarely the focus. In families, this might look like showing Dad how to care for and fix Baby Girl's hair. He may not ever be a technical expert, but he will at least know enough to make it through picture day if he is for some reason left alone when that day comes.

This idea of hiring for the tough stuff is where alignment with your vision and values comes in as well. It can be challenging to find someone who shares your vision for the business and the values by which you operate. Although they may possess adequate technical knowledge, if they aren't operating as you imagined, it could be difficult to watch your company change. In some cases, this may be okay. If your vision and values are a critical component of your business, you will want to begin filling your pipeline with people who share yours. This could happen by seeking them out and spending substantial time with them, or it can happen through the "grooming" process. Over time, people can buy into your vision and values and take them on as their own. This is often the case when family members are taking over. Over time (as in the rearing process), you have the opportunity to instill a set of values that, ideally, they would carry with them into the business. They can also catch your vision along the way, but it does take time.

In addition to developing technical skills and growing commitment to the values, soft skills cannot be overlooked. If your successor is a family member, you have a wonderful opportunity to begin developing that person's soft skills early. Soft skills include those knowledge, skills, and abilities that are more difficult to train or learn. They include characteristics such as communication skills, interpersonal skills, critical thinking, positive attitude, learning aptitude, leadership, persuasion, etc. These are skills that apply across functional or technical areas. From my previous examples of leadership being hired or identified by their soft skills and trained in the technical skills, can you see why an organization would want to do that? It is much easier to teach someone a specific system or technical knowledge than to teach them how to care about people. This is why advocates push so hard for educators to focus on critical thinking and problem solving over memorizing books of information. Depending on your succession approach, you may have the ability to hire or select based on these soft skills. In many cases, though, you may need time to develop them. As important as the technical side may be, the soft skills are equally as important for long-term success.

All of this preparation is great, but how will you know if the people and processes you are putting in place will actually work? An important and often overlooked part of the succession planning process is actually stepping away. Take a step back from your family or business for a day, a week, a month, and see how it operates. This is often referred to as the "stress test". The idea is to put your business or family under stress, which often happens when you aren't there, and won't be there to save it. This allows you to see how things would fare without you there.

Managers are often reluctant to take that step back and trust their teams. They swoop in when there's a problem and save the day. What they're actually doing is handicapping the very ones who may one day be responsible for running the entire operation. By not putting trust in your team, by not giving them the opportunity to grow, learn, and make mistakes, you are not being a leader; you are simply a manager.

If you want to create a true succession plan filled with a pipeline of people who you trust to carry your business into the next generation, you must let them lead while you are still there. Take that anniversary trip, take a step back and focus only on content for a week, take a month-long sabbatical. Give your team the tools and resources to run the business and tell them not to contact you unless it is an emergency. A *true* emergency. Give them a chance to fail, and give them a chance to succeed. It is only through making mistakes and having hiccups that we learn how to do it better next time.

I'm not just promoting this type of experiment with your business. I encourage moms to do this as well. Go out to dinner with your friends, leave the house on a Saturday, take a weekend for yourself, hand off the bills for a month. Not only will you feel more relaxed and rejuvenated, but you will give your husband a chance to prove to you, and himself, that he really can handle the bedtime routine alone. You will both feel better as a result. Of course, this scenario can easily be flipped. Dads often do activities that moms know little about. Do you know how to call on the refrigerator warranty or where to get the oil changed? Can you show your son how to change a tire if needed? If Dad pays the bills, could you pick up that responsibility? I don't mean to imply that women do it all and dads are deadbeats. I know that may be the case, but for most of us, there are things we each need to learn from the other. These are just a few, potentially stereotypical examples.

Before I wrap up this section, I want to touch on one thing you might be wondering. Some of you may question why a succession plan is necessary at all. Especially if you struggle with seeing your business as a business rather than a hobby. Unless your business is truly a hobby for your own pleasure and enjoyment, then it is probably providing an important service or ministry to others. A little planning can help ensure that the hard work you put into it will continue blessing others for years to come. Don't devalue your effort by thinking it's not worth a little foresight. Ultimately, you may decide that it isn't necessary. When you are ready to move on, you can honestly say it's okay if your business moves on as well. If that is truly the case, then you may not need a complex succession plan. I do still encourage you to have that plan for any unexpected situations where you are unable to properly shut down your business. If you were suddenly unable to run your business, for whatever reason, what would be the repercussions of that? What programs or tools would be automatically auto-renewed each year (i.e., websites, domain names, software)? Who would need to be notified? How would they be notified? Who has access to your business accounts? Regardless of whether or not you have any desire to transfer your business, there are certain things that you should document.

Well, that was a bit of a negative ending, but succession planning tends to be a little on the rough side. It can, though, be a very liberating and positive experience as you make plans to keep your business alive or know that you are making the transition process a little smoother for those you love. I encourage you to take some time to think through your plan and take a small action every day to move in that direction.

Summary:

- If your business has value outside of your own enjoyment, it is probably important enough to think through a succession plan.

- Certain processes and information can be documented along the way to make the transition smoother while technical knowledge and values often need to be developed over time.

- A succession plan is essential for supporting those who may be left to shut down your business for you.

THIS IS THEN

Myth 19: I'm not living my purpose yet. *Once* I (leave my job, get the children into school/graduated, drop fifty pounds, win the lottery), then I will fulfill my purpose.

Truth 19: Whatever you are doing, you can fulfill your purpose right then, right there, right now. *This* is *then*.

So many times, I have talked to women who were living their dreams or at least a part of them, but they weren't enjoying it. They didn't recognize it as their dreams because of unmet expectations. I am passionate about helping women to not only live the life of their dreams but also to love it. I recognize, though, that not everyone is yet living the life of their dreams. Perhaps you are still working a full-time j-o-b and haven't quite begun to follow your passion. Perhaps you are a stay-at-home mom watching a house full of little ones waiting to start a small business or go back to work that you love. Maybe you are at home full time *and* working a part-time job or side hustle that doesn't necessarily align with your overall goals but is necessary right now. Perhaps you are single and want nothing more than to get married and start, or continue, your family. Whatever the case, you may feel that this book or these principles don't apply to you because you just aren't there yet.

I want to encourage you that you are *exactly* where you are supposed to be. For years, and I do mean years, I thought I was wasting time. I knew I wasn't where God ultimately wanted me, and I certainly wasn't doing what God had uniquely equipped me to do. I was struggling with taking the leap, but as my own sole provider, I couldn't exactly jump ship. I suggested moving in with my parents so I could meet my full potential full-time, but they weren't digging that idea. Unfortunately, I wasted those years waiting for the time to be right. Instead of spending that time learning, growing, and building the foundation for my next step, I spent all of my energy questioning why God hadn't opened certain doors for me. I waited for the right promotion to line up, the right supervisor to recognize my skills, and the right doors to be shut. Several years ago, I finally started to get the message. "Grow where you're planted". I saw that message over and over.

During one of my devotionals, I was bartering with God. "If you would just give me a chance with one event planner, *then* I would be able to share your message. If you would just get me one consulting contract, *then* I would have time to devote more energy to fulfilling your purpose for my life. If you would just help me get in front of one agent, *then* I would be able to make a real difference in the lives of women. God, as soon as I drop fifty pounds and feel more comfortable in my body, *then* I will be able to move forward." I wanted to go places. I wanted to do big things, but people and circumstances in my way were just roadblocks. What I was currently doing was just a roadblock. My children (the very people I was doing it for), my j-o-b (the thing that was building my skills), the student asking for advice, the people walking to their cars after the conference. I just wanted to yell, "Can you see I'm trying to help people?! I wish everyone would just get out of my way!" I was so focused on the end that I forgot that what really mattered was the journey. As I was complaining to Him about His performance, I heard very clearly, "Cheryl. This *is* then. Why are you waiting? I put you here for a reason. This is exactly where I want you, and you can fulfill your purpose right here and right now. Why do you think I put all of these people in your path? Why do you think I put you in this place right now? *this* is what it's all about."

How on earth could I have missed that for so long? Logically I understood that life was a journey and to grow where I was planted, but it never really sunk in until that moment. I didn't need some grand gesture or some full-time adventure of passion. I could fulfill His purpose for my life *through* my day j-o-b, *during* my commute, and *while* shopping at the grocery store. His purpose for our lives is very clear and very consistent. Our role is to share Him with the world. That's it. Whether we are running our own business or commuting to a cubicle every day, our purpose does not change. He does want us to be happy, but happiness is not the ultimate goal. Our mission is to bring glory to God. It may be the case that you aren't doing what you love full-time just yet. I do believe in my heart of hearts that if God gave you the desire, you will get there. I want you to take comfort, though, in the fact that you did not miss your purpose. It may look different than you thought it would, but you are doing it. Every time you speak with love to your children - you are doing it. Every time you give grace to a person who cut you off on the highway - you are doing it. Whenever you give a smile to someone on the street - you are doing it. It may not be how you would have chosen, but God is still faithful. He says, "Give it to me. Come as you are. I can use you right now." Trust that He is working behind the scenes to beautifully knit together the masterpiece of your life. Keep trusting that and walk in obedience. You are learning lessons, touching lives, and laying the foundation for the next step He is preparing for you. Regardless of how far you think you have strayed, know that by walking in His word daily, you are fulfilling His purpose for your life right now.

I saw a meme on Facebook that read, "I love how being an adult is just saying, *But after this week things will slow down a bit again*, to yourself until you die." We laugh about it because it is so true! Unfortunately, we often apply this same logic to chasing our dreams. "When things slow down a bit," has become our mantra. When your "when" statement starts to get to you, and you think that only "then" can you be who God made you to be, I want you to ask yourself what is the *very next* thing you can do *right now* to get you to where you want to be. Dropping fifty pounds is not the *very next* thing. It's a project. The very next thing you can do to meet that goal is to choose to eat a grilled chicken sandwich instead of a fried chicken sandwich. Once you have made that choice, get back to your computer and do the very next thing you need to do to get you to your goal. That may be writing three pages, contacting a planner, or reaching out to a lead. It is not setting up a dating profile, cleaning off your desk, or looking at plans for your dream home. Despite what you might think, you do *not* have to wait for something to change in order to start reaching your goals now. Sometimes we get wrapped up in the big displays of faithfulness that we forget the importance of the small steps.

We live in a world of doubt and fear. Even when we truly believe we heard God speak to us, we doubt. What if I heart wrong? What if this is just what I want to do and not what God is *telling* me to do? What if this was just a test and I messed it up? I know these fears all too well and spent the majority of my life darting from one door to the next hoping to magically land in the right doorway. It makes me laugh now because that is such a small vision of our God. He is so much bigger than my choices. My family rented a boat one summer and went out on the lake. We parked in a small cove and jumped in the water. The boat floated more than it should have and started to encroach on the rocks. As hard as we tried to maneuver the boat, at idle, it was at the mercy of the waves. It wasn't until we turned on the boat that we could maneuver away from the rocks. Just like you can't steer a sitting ship, you can't change direction if you aren't moving. You must take those first steps in faith. Only then can God nudge you in the direction He is calling you.

I was telling God about how I would drop everything for His will if that's what he wanted. "I will sell my house and live in an RV. I will give up Facebook for the rest of my life. I will never make another unnecessary purchase again. Whatever you want; I will do it." I sat for a long time just listening in anticipation of the big reveal. I couldn't wait to hear what God wanted me to do in order to show Him how devoted I was. I couldn't wait to be a martyr for my faith. I started to hear whispers. "Spend time with me every morning: First thing in the morning." Okay. Well, that's not asking a lot. What else? "Stop eating sugar." Okay. That's a lot, but it's pretty simple. I'll stop eating flour too, and never eat again after seven, and do Keto, and set a record for the most weight loss in a single day. "No. Just sugar. For ninety days. That's it. Stop eating sugar and don't expect dramatic results." Okay. Fine. Just sugar. Ninety days. No expectations. What else? Anything big? Exciting? Martyr-y? "That's it. Just spend time with me and stop eating all of that junk. Show me you can be faithful in these things, and I'll give you more." It is sometimes hard to hear that our big purpose is to take small steps. It feels so slow and small, but it is sometimes the small steps that God uses to do big things. It is also the small steps where we must remain the most obedient and faithful. When the music stops and the crowds die down, when the attention has turned elsewhere and we are left with trusting God alone, *that* is when our faith is tested the most.

Running a business or your family is tough. There isn't a guide-book for doing life just right. Being successful requires a great deal of trial, error, persistence, and above all, faithfulness. My hope is that you have picked up a few tips that you can begin implementing in your family or business today. Although it isn't necessarily easy, it doesn't always have to be so hard. You were made to do great things! I pray that the ideas within these pages give you a bit of confidence to step into who you were made to be. Life is the sum of the steps you take every day. Don't wait until things are easier, slower, or better to start living your dreams. The time is now. God didn't put you on this earth to wait until the children are out of school. He doesn't care that you would like to drop twenty, fifty, or 100 pounds. He has asked you to move and trust him. Will you take that leap of faith today and just start walking?

"Trust in the Lord with all your heart and lean not on your own understanding; in all your ways submit to Him, and he will make your paths straight." Proverbs 3:5-6 NIV

Summary:

- You can fulfill your purpose right now.

- Life is the sum of the steps you take every day.

- When things don't make sense, just keep walking in faith.

A NOTE FROM CHERYL

I hope that you have enjoyed taking a peek into the world of Big Business. It is my prayer that you are able to take something from this book that will help you regain the joy in your business and family. When the wheels are coming off, it can be difficult to enjoy even the greatest blessings in our lives. I pray that you will be able to implement a few of the practices outlined in this book and regain a bit of that sanity that you may have lost along the way.

Please forgive me for being a terrible example when it comes to properly citing my references. If you are interested in the citations, I will be happy to send those to you. Given that they are not properly cited according to the most recent APA standards, I have opted to hide in shame, providing them only to those interested enough to ask.

I would love to hear about the incredible things you are doing and how these techniques may have encouraged you to achieve more than you thought possible. It is these stories that encourage me to continue to do what I do, so please don't keep them to yourself! Time is the greatest gift you can give someone. Thank you for trusting me enough to give me some of your precious time by reading this book. I pray you consider it a worthy investment in your future!

ENDNOTES

1. Self-Discipline. (2019). In Oxford Learner's Dictionaries. Retrieved from
    https://www.oxfordlearnersdictionaries.com/us/definition/english/self-discipline

2. Lipton, B.H. (2016). The Biology of Belief. Carlsbad, CA: Hay House, Inc.

3. Return to Now (2017). 85% of People Hate Their Jobs, Gallup Poll Says. Retrieved from https://returntonow.net/2017/09/22/85-people-hate-jobs-gallup-poll-says/

4. Britz, M. (2018). Don't think training first for employee development. Business Journal (Central New York), 32(18), 5B-6B.

5. Unalienable. (2019) In Dictionary.com. Retrieved from https://www.dictionary.com/browse/unalienable

6. Hamilton, C. (2008). Why did Jefferson change "property" to the "pursuit of happiness"? Columbia College of Arts and Sciences Human News Network. Retrieved from http://hnn.us/articles/46460.html

7. Happiness. (2019). Bing search powered by Oxford Dictionaries. Retrieved from https://www.bing.com/search?q=happiness+definition&form=PRLNC1&src=IE11TR&pc=EUPP_LCTE

8. Happiness. (2019). Encyclopedia Britannica. Retrieved from https://www.britannica.com/topic/happiness

9. Tumen, S., and Tugba Z. (2015) Is Happiness Contagious? Separating Spillover Externalities from the Group-Level Social Context. Journal of Happiness Studies. 16, no. 3 (June 2015): 719–44.

10. Cacioppo, J. T., Fowler, J. H., & Christakis, N. A. (2009). Alone in the Crowd: The Structure and Spread of Loneliness in a Large Social Network. Journal of Personality & Social Psychology, [s. l.], v. 97, n. 6, p. 977–99.

11. Kellogg School of Management (2017). Sitting Near a High-Performer Can Make You Better at Your Job. Thrive Global. Retrieved from https://medium.com/thrive-global/how-sitting-near-a-high-performer-can-make-you-better-at-your-job-825f1699c29b

12. Hyatt, M. (2019). Free to Focus. Ada, MI: Baker Publishing Group.

13. Goman, C.K. (2018). How Women Can Escape The Impostor Syndrome Trap. Forbes Magazine. (May 2018). Retrieved from https://www.forbes.com/sites/carolkinseygoman/2018/05/17/how-women-can-escape-the-imposter-syndrome-trap/#1a0a77cf489b

14. Rath, T. (2007). StrengthsFinder 2.0. New York, NY: Gallup Press.

15. Mark, G., Gudith, D., & Klocke, U. (2008). The cost of interrupted work: more speed and stress. Retrieved from https://www.ics.uci.edu/~gmark/chi08-mark.pdf

16. Hohlbaum, C.L. (2009). The Power of Slow: 101 Ways to Save Time in Our 24/7. New York: NY: St. Martin's Press. Quote retrieved from https://psychcentral.com/blog/5-ways-to-prevent-job-burnout/

17. Tartakovsky, M. (2018) 5 Ways to Prevent Burnout. Retrieved from https://psychcentral.com/blog/5-ways-to-prevent-job-burnout/

ABOUT THE AUTHOR

Dr. Cheryl LeJewell Jackson lives in Texas with her husband, two precious boys, and as much family as one house can hold. After earning her Doctorate in Industrial-Organizational Psychology, she traveled the country working with organizations and helping employees find fulfillment at work. Family brought her back to her hometown where she enjoys encouraging women to step into who they were made to be through writing, speaking, and inspiring employees in the workplace. Cheryl stays active in the field and in her community by running her own consulting company, teaching in the graduate program at the local university, playing flute in her church orchestra, and serving on the board of directors for a local food pantry.

www.ingramcontent.com/pod-product-compliance
Lightning Source LLC
Chambersburg PA
CBHW030617220526
45463CB00004B/1324